D1201304

Ben Franklin
in
Paris

Ben Franklin

in

Paris

Play and Lyrics by

SIDNEY MICHAELS

Music by

MARK SANDRICH, JR.

Random House: New York

MANUFACTURED IN THE UNITED STATES OF AMERICA

To Louisette—the Happiness I Pursue

A Few Words about History

Historically, Ben Franklin was seventy-plus years old when he did nearly all the things that are recorded in this play, but dramatically no one would believe it, so the character is meant to be played in his romantic fifties, as a concession to the realism of fiction which life hasn't got time for. Age is never specified in the play so you are free to think of him as seventy-plus if you are somebody to whom the incredible is easy.

Franklin never, so far as we know, ascended in a balloon, as he does in this play; but he surely must have ascended in his imagination often, for he eagerly advised those floating astronauts in their wickerwork rockets, observed with ardor the first Cape Kennedy in the Bois de Boulogne, prophesied the future warring employment thereof—and the planes, the bombs and the devastation of great cities. And his understanding has been reported to us: When asked "Whatever is the use of it?" he responded, "Whatever is the use of a baby?"

But the details of the balloon scene in the play are unimagined. They come straight from a first-person contemporary account: the fear of sparks catching in the silk, the fueling of the stove with packets of straw, the narrow escape from coming down in the river, and the going aloft of amateurs—ladies included, and often with a picnic lunch, the life-and-limb balloon becoming the eighteenth century's back seat of the life-and-limb family car that Dad loaned Sonny on a Saturday night.

One of the critics pointed out in his review of *Ben Franklin* that while he doubted Dr. Franklin disembarked in France carting a luggage of his famous inventions, he, the critic, was nonetheless delighted to see them paraded upon the stage, sufficiently excused by the freedoms of musical comedy. I am sorry to report that this was not a case of dramatic license: Ben actually took all his inventions to Paris for good old Madison Avenue purposes of propaganda, to advertise his Cause, and as gifts for the influential. The canny Doctor had a carny bent.

Now, it may be interesting to show an example of Ben's writing as he wrote it in 1785, and then that same matter as it became transformed into dialogue in a musical play written about him in 1964. Here is Ben's account of his invention of the bifocals:

> . . . I therefore had formerly two pair of spectacles, which I shifted occasionally, as in traveling I sometimes read, and often wanted to regard the prospects. Finding this change troublesome, and not always sufficiently ready, I had the glasses cut, and half of each kind associated in the same circle.
>
> By this means, as I wear my spectacles constantly, I have only to move my eyes up or down, as I want to see distinctly far or near. . . .

And here is the same account as I altered it for *Ben Franklin in Paris*:

> BEN (*He takes a pair of spectacles out of his pocket and goes to* DIANE) Compliments of the Continental Congress—a pair of bifocals.
>
> DIANE Bifocals?

BEN I invented them because I thought a man should be able to see the girl in his arms at one and the same time as her husband coming in at the far door.

DIANE But there is nothing wrong with my eyesight, Monsieur.

BEN Well, you see France's problems under your nose, Madame. But what of her great advantages which lie three thousand miles away, where together we could smash the British Empire! No, Madame, your eyesight is right as rain; 'tis your insight that needs the bifocals.

Historically, there were four ladies, where the play compresses them to one, because four physically consummated affairs carried on simultaneously at seventy-plus, or fifty, might on the stage appear foolish, whereas in life they were engaged in with the greatest seriousness of affection.

The somewhat curious maternal relationship between Madame la Comtesse and the King is a dramatic approximation of truth which might strike the audience as something not truth. The fact is that Louis XVI required a very delicate operation to enable him to enjoy any physically consummated affair and since, with good reason, he feared the surgical skills of his day, all his relationships at this time were platonic. A few years later, he underwent a circumcision and his wife, Marie Antoinette, proceeded to bear him four children.

Marie Antoinette is not introduced during the course of this play because she was at this time only sixteen years old and not very much concerned with Franklin's mission.

Her only encounter with Franklin was at the gambling tables, where her advice served the great man's cause only in that it cost him money and probably made his position even more desperate than it was before. This may be construed as a factor in urging him on, but scarcely of sufficient importance to include it.

Even a show that was blessed with four rave reviews leaves its author with certain second thoughts; and one of what I consider my grossest failures in this show was the underdeveloped use of Beaumarchais. This was at the widest variance with the facts, for I employed him as Ben's confidant; but in actuality, Ben has been reported to have held Beau in very low esteem, finding him too shallow, devious, flippant and foppish for Ben's taste, which was homespun taste, handmade on the edge of a wilderness as alien to the French court as is the terrain of the moon to us today. There was a better confidant to be used: Edward Bancroft, Ben's London crony who came and lived with the Americans at Passy and was discovered, a hundred years later, to have been, all the time, the head of the British espionage. But to use Bancroft would be to steal thunder, come the second act, from the already quite complex set of climaxes which the story demanded—namely, the turning traitor of Ben's son, and the return of the spinning wheel from the Countess, signifying the exhaustion of Ben's resourcefulness and the resultant decision to lay his life on the line, in a gesture of idealism foreign to his nature. Not to mention the necessity to tie up the tale of shy Temple's romance with the forthright Janine and his finally standing up to Ben and telling him to go to hell. Had Beaumarchais been given a subplot of his own, for in actual fact, it was greatly Beau's doing that moneys were borrowed, guns purchased, and the battle of Saratoga won, such a chain of events might have zippered all the other plots together into a snugger fit. Sic transit planning.

I read in the paper the other day that some scientists believe that any sound ever made continues to exist in the air and that they have, even now, a machine which has managed to pick up conversations in a room which are a week old. Ah, to pick up Shakespeare in a heated debate with Burbage! Or, for that matter, to pick up Ben the night he stayed till dawn at Mme. Brillon's while she bathed naked in a slipper tub or the day he sat down with the twenty-one-year-old Jefferson and blue-penciled the Declaration of Independence, adding the phrase, as we know he did, "We hold these truths to be self-evident"! Still, it may be preferable to relish the fantastic notion than to ever achieve it. For it is never the accuracy of history that is its glory, so much as it is what the future makes of it in the light of the present. I tried to be guided that way in the writing of *Ben*. Not the letter but the spirit.

At any rate, I gave to Beau, Bancroft's confidancy, and to Ben, Beau's activity, and I represented Ben's distaste for Beau, which was unfair, by a mild jibe about Beau's ripping his velvet britches on a picket fence were he to follow Lafayette to the American War.

Here is a "pick-up" of Ben's own "Advice to a Young Man on the Choosing of a Mistress":

. . . In all your amours you should prefer old women to young ones.

You call this a paradox and demand my reasons. They are these:

1. Because they have more knowledge of the world, and their minds are better stored with observations, their conversation is more improving and more lastingly agreeable.

2. Because when women cease to be handsome they study to be good. To maintain their influence over men, they supply the diminution of beauty by an augmentation of utility. They learn to do a thousand services small and great, and are the most tender and useful of friends when you are sick. Thus they continue amiable. And hence there is hardly such a thing to be found as an old woman who is not a good woman.

3. Because there is no hazard of children, which irregularly produced may be attended with much inconvenience.

4. Because through more experience they are more prudent and discreet in conducting an intrigue to prevent suspicion. The commerce with them is therefore safer with regard to your reputation. And with regard to theirs, if the affair should happen to be known, considerate people might be rather inclined to excuse an old woman, who would kindly take care of a young man, form his manners by her good counsels, and prevent his ruining his health & fortune among mercenary prostitutes.

5. Because in every animal that walks upright the deficiency of the fluids that fill the muscles appears first in the highest part. The face first grows lank and wrinkled; then the neck; then the breast and arms; the lower parts continuing to the last as plump as ever: so that covering all above with a basket, and regarding only what is below the girdle, it is impossible of two women to tell an old one from a young one. And as in the dark all cats are gray, the pleasure of corporal enjoyment with an old woman is at least equal, and frequently superior; every knack being, by practice, capable of improvement.

6. Because the sin is less. The debauching of a
virgin may be her ruin, and make her for life un-
happy.

7. Because the compunction is less. The having
made a young girl miserable may give you frequent
bitter reflection; none of which can attend the making an old woman happy.

8. And lastly. They are so grateful!!

And here is what it became in the light of a later day:

BEN Come here. (TEMPLE *sits near* BEN *on the
sofa*) You ever notice how a dog gets ready to lie
down on a rug?

TEMPLE Yes, sir.

BEN Well, before a man settles down, Temple, he
ought to turn about a bit . . . look around. Explore
avenues.

TEMPLE Sir?

BEN For experience.

TEMPLE You mean . . .

BEN I do, sir. And an older woman is preferable to a
younger one.

TEMPLE You're not serious.

BEN I am! Why, they can educate you and keep
you off the streets, and in no way is the pleasure
any less. For in every animal that walks upright,

the body ages from the top down, you know. Leaving the lowermost plump and fetching to the last. You can take the clothes off an old woman and the clothes off a young woman, and put a basket over the head of each and I defy you to tell me which is which.

TEMPLE (*Rises . . .*) Good God, sir. How do you know?

BEN Hearsay. And last but not least . . . they are so grateful!

TEMPLE But if everyone were to take up with older women, sir, what would younger women do?

BEN Take up with older men, Temple. Take up with older men!

It is a little odd that a musical play is published without the presence of one half of its creative authorship. For in the "person" of a musical play, the play part is its body and the music is its soul. Though it is the fad these days to lay undue emphasis on a "strong book," when all is said and done, it is my firm belief that a musical is still its music. That is certainly true of *Ben*, but lyric and text are published by book publishers and score is published by music publishers. Perhaps the problem is an educational one. Were a civilized society to teach children how to read and write music as it does language, insisting on musicology as on literacy, the lovely melodies of Mark Sandrich, Jr., might be printed here along with the words that led up to and accompanied them, and the reader would hear, as he read, the vigorous urgent rhythm of "I Invented Myself," the stirring pride of "Half the Battle," the saucy bounce of "Hic Haec Hoc," the bittersweet of "How Laughable It Is," and the rich, warm, gentle humanity of "Look for Small Pleasures."

These adjectives are all qualities as equally possessed by the composer himself as by his compositions. The theater is the Art of Collaboration, and a composer for the stage is a playwright whose words are notes, and whose thoughts are melodies. Only half the play is here and anyone who owns this book should provide himself with the Capitol Records show album. The latter has enjoyed an unusually large sale and therefore I equally hope that anyone who owns the record will provide himself with this book. Perhaps it might be interesting to see how one of Ben's bagatelles found itself turned into a song. Here is his letter to the Abbé Morellet about the happy accident of the human elbow:

> . . . To confirm you still more in your piety and recognition of Divine Providence, reflect upon the position which He has given to the elbow. Animals which have to drink the water that flows upon the earth, if they have long legs have also long necks, in order that they may reach their drinking without the trouble of kneeling. But man, who was destined to drink wine, ought to be able to carry the glass to his mouth. If the elbow had been placed nearer the hand, the forearm would have been too short to bring the glass to the mouth; if it had been placed nearer the shoulder, the rest of the arm would have been so long, that it would have carried the glass quite beyond the mouth; thus would we have been tantalized. But owing to the present position we are able to drink at our ease, the glass coming exactly to the mouth. Let

us adore then, glass in hand, this benevolent wisdom; let us adore and drink.

And alas, here is but the naked verse I made of it, without the attractive vestments of the music with which Mr. Sandrich clothed it:

> Gentlemen, I give you the elbow.
> A neglected annex of the arm,
> A practical piece of poetry, sirs.
> A tough hide covering a thing of lovely
> Flexibility.
>
> That flowers should grow is no wonder at all
> For the seed and the soil make it obvious
> To any.
>
> But that there should flourish
> Between the shoulders and the wrists
> That surprising joint of joints
> Is a matter for philosophers to ponder.
>
> For, gentlemen, when all is said and done,
> What is it, after all, with which one tests
> A baby's bath?
>
> (Sings)
> God bless the human elbow,
> God bless it where it bends.
> If it bent too long,
> We'd be dry I fear:
> If it bent too short,
> We'd be drinking through our ear,

But
It bends just right,
In the middle of the arm,
Not too loose, not too tight,
As we lean on it each night,
With a well-oiled kind of charm.

When the brain won't tick,
When the heart won't leap,
When the stomach feels sick,
When the foot's asleep,
Then, we point man and boy,
As its wonders we employ
To that luckily knuckling, anatomical joy.

People may leap to the conclusion that the author's invention begins with such things as Ben's having a servant whose name is Jacques Finque and who stole the kitchen funds. I confess it is unlikely but it is absolutely accurate. Perhaps this is the origin of the word "fink."

I left out the fact that Ben's marriage to his late wife, Debby, was illegitimate as she had been already married to somebody else at the time; that Ben's son Bill was illegitimate; that Bill's son Temple was illegitimate and that Temple's son was illegitimately born to the French girl represented in this play by Janine. Not that I think it isn't interesting, just that audiences won't sit for ten hours at a musical and something had to go.

And then Dr. Franklin wrote, in 1773:

I have seen an instance of common flies . . . drowned in Madeira wine, apparently about the time when it was bottled in Virginia, to be sent here (to London). At the opening of one of the bottles, at the house of a friend where I was, three drowned flies fell into the first glass that was filled. Having heard it remarked that drowned flies came back to life in the sun, I proposed making the experiment upon these. They were therefore exposed to the sun upon a sieve which had been employed to strain them out of the wine. In less than three hours, two of them began by degrees to recover life. They commenced by some convulsive motions in the thighs, and at length they raised themselves upon their legs, wiped their eyes with their fore feet, beat and brushed their wings with their hind feet, and soon after flew away, finding themselves in Old England, without knowing how they came thither. The third continued lifeless till sun-set, when, losing all hopes of him, he was thrown away.

I wish it were possible, from this instance, to invent a method of embalming drowned persons, in such a manner that they might be recalled to life at any period, however distant; for having a very ardent desire to see and observe the state of America an hundred years hence, I should prefer to an ordinary death, the being immersed with a few friends in a cask of Madeira, until that time, then to be recalled to life by the solar warmth of my dear country! . . .

Which formed the basis for the soliloquy at the end of *Ben Franklin in Paris* which I will not here provide in order to be sure you read from here to there, if only out of curiosity as to what was made of it. And cursed be he who skips!

The most often asked questions I have had about this play are the following: Did Ben's son really turn traitor? Did Ben really tell dirty jokes? Did Ben really get a man drunk to acquire his guns? Did Ben really propose marriage to a French countess? Did Ben really try to matchmake his grandson with French nobility? Did Ben really expect to be our first President? Did Ben really entertain letting the British hang him for the effect of martyrdom? Did the final scene of the play literally happen as presented? The answer to all is, Yes. All of these incredible things are true.

The easiest thing would have been to make an old-fashioned farce out of this material but the easiest thing is never as worth doing as the hardest thing.

S.R.M.

Ben Franklin in Paris *was first presented by George W. George and Frank Granat on October 27, 1964, at the Lunt-Fontanne Theatre, New York City, with the following cast:*

(In order of appearance)

CAPTAIN WICKES	Sam Greene
BENJAMIN FRANKLIN	Robert Preston
TEMPLE FRANKLIN	Franklin Kiser
BENJAMIN FRANKLIN BACHE	Jerry Schaefer
FOOTMAN	Anthony Falco
LOUIS XVI	Oliver Clark
VERGENNES	Art Bartow
TURGOT	Clifford Fearl
MADAME LA COMTESSE DIANE DE VOBRILLAC	Ulla Sallert
BRITISH GRENADIER	Roger LePage
DAVID LORD STORMONT	Byron Webster
FRENCH SOLDIER	Ron Schwinn
PIERRE CARON DE BEAUMARCHAIS	Bob Kaliban
JACQUES FINQUE	John Taliaferro
LITTLE BOY	Stuart Getz
PEDRO COUNT DE ARANDA	Jack Fletcher
BOOKSELLER	Herb Mazzini
JANINE NICOLET	Susan Watson
ABBÉ DE MORELLET	Herb Mazzini
SPANISH AIDE-DE-CAMP	Kip Andrews
SPANISH SOLDIER	Art Matthews
SPANISH AMBASSADOR'S DAUGHTER	Suzanne France
YVONNE	Lauren Jones

SINGERS and DANCERS

Barbara Bossert, Mona Crawford, Hilda Harris, Anita Maye, Caroline Parks, Art Bartow, Anthony Falco, Clifford Fearl, John Keatts, Art Matthews, Herb Mazzini, John Taliaferro, Diane Ball, Marilyn Charles, Jean Eliot, Suzanne France, Ellen Graff, Lauren Jones, Sandy Roveta, Kip Andrews, Roger LePage, George Ramos, Eddie Roll, Rec Russel, Ron Schwinn, Lou Zeldis.

Directed and choreographed by MICHAEL KIDD

Production designed by OLIVER SMITH

Costumes designed by MOTLEY

Lighting by JACK BROWN

Orchestrations by PHILIP J. LANG

Musical Direction and Vocal Arrangements by
DONALD PIPPIN

Dance Music by ROGER ADAMS

SYNOPSIS OF SCENES

The entire action takes place in France—1776-1777.

ACT ONE

Prologue
1. The Docks
2. The Throne Room at Versailles
3. Paristown
4. Ben's House
5. Promenade
6. The Park
7. Sky over Paris
8. The Pont Neuf
9. Paristown
10. Ben's House
11. The Cloisters
12. The Winery

ACT TWO

1. The Spanish Embassy
2. A Corridor at Versailles
3. Diane's House
4. Outside Ben's House
5. Ben's House
6. A Corridor at Versailles
7. The Throne Room at Versailles

MUSICAL NUMBERS

ACT ONE

"We Sail the Seas"	American Marines
"I Invented Myself"	Ben and Company
"Too Charming"	Ben, Diane
"Whatever Became of Old Temple"	Temple
"Half the Battle"	Ben, Benny, Temple, Beaumarchais
"A Balloon Is Ascending"	Company
"To Be Alone with You"	Ben, Diane and Company
"You're in Paris"	Janine, Temple and Company
"How Laughable It Is"	Diane
"Hic Haec Hoc"	Monks
"God Bless the Human Elbow"	Ben, Pedro, Beaumarchais and Monks

ACT TWO

"When I Dance with the Person I Love"	Janine
"Diane Is"	Ben
"Look for Small Pleasures"	Ben, Diane
"I Love the Ladies"	Ben, Captain Wickes, Beaumarchais, Temple and Marines
"To Be Alone with You" (Reprise)	Ben

Act One

Prologue

Winter, 1776. It is dawn at sea. The scene is in the tops aboard the S.S. Reprisal. The U.S. Marine Corps was created to guard DR. FRANKLIN *on his journey to Paris; and five* MARINES *search the horizon for the landfall. They sing "We Sail the Seas."*

MARINE ONE
> We hail from Massachusetts, old New Hamp, the
> Carolines,

MARINE TWO
> Rhode Island and Connecticut,

MARINE THREE
> Georgia, Jersey, and New York,

MARINE FOUR
> Pennsylvanie, Maryland, Virginie, Delaware;
> Boys who sail the seas to freedom.

MARINE FIVE
> We come from where there's corn on the cob,
> And plenty of tasseled wheat,

ALL
> Where the sun is piled

3

So that every child
Can live on a gold-paved street.

MARINE ONE
We come from where there's apples to bob,
And a crown is the top of your hat,

ALL
And turkey runs wild
So that every child
Can grow up to be as natural free as that.

We hail from Massachusetts, old New Hamp, the
    Carolines,
Rhode Island and Connecticut, Georgia, Jersey, and
    New York,
Pennsylvanie, Maryland, Virginie, Delaware;
Boys who sail the seas to freedom.

MARINE TWO   Hey, what's that?

MARINE THREE   That's French cooking smoke!

MARINE FOUR (*Sighting land*)   Quiberon Bay! There she
    is! France to starboard!

MARINE FIVE   Don't tread on me!

MARINE ONE   We'll turn the world upside down!

MARINE TWO   Hear, hear, Your Majesty! Bonnie jour!
        (*A rope is thrown to the ship and is hauled across
        the stage as the good* Reprisal *docks. The lights go*

4

down and come up as the rope is now pulled in the
other direction by French hands on land)

ALL

We hail from Massachusetts, old New Hamp,
The Carolines, Rhode Island and Connecticut,
Georgia, Jersey and New York.
Pennsylvanie, Maryland, Virginie, Delaware.
Boys who sail,
Boys who sail,
Boys who sail the seas to freedom!

Blackout

Scene One

The bells peal. A CROWD *has gathered.* FRANKLIN's *rocking chair, printing press, lightning rods, stove, kite and baggage are brought off the ship. Down the gangplank* BENJAMIN FRANKLIN *enters wearing a fur-collared coat, beaver cap and with a crab apple walking stick.*

BEN (*Vigorously*) Good morning to you all! I've got to catch the coach to Paris and I'm in a blasted hurry!

SHOPKEEPER Ah, Monsieur le Docteur, how goes the revolution?

BEN Brilliantly!

WENCH But we hear you retreat!

BEN Brilliantly!

BAKER'S BOY Ah, Monsieur le Docteur, are you come for recognition?

BEN No, no, I've come for my health and the education of my grandchildren. Where are they? (TEMPLE FRANKLIN, BEN's *seventeen-year-old grandson, and* BENJAMIN FRANKLIN BACHE, *his seven-year-old grandson, come down the gangplank. They are cousins*) Bundle up,

6

Benny. It's still winter out. (*To the* CROWD) Mr. Temple Franklin, my son's son and my secretary. Master Benjamin Franklin Bache, my daughter's boy. (*To the* MARINES) Why am I here, lads?

MARINES (*As if memorized*) "For his health and the education of his grandchildren!"

BEN (*Grinning*) That's the absolute truth, because if I don't get the recognition my health is going to be shot to hell and that's the end of their education.
(*The* CROWD *laughs*)

TEMPLE (*Horrified*) Grandfather! Congress made you swear not to—

BEN Nonsense! Everybody knows we're in trouble.
(*A* BOY *wheels a bicycle into view—it has no pedals.* BEN *leaps forward, eagerly, totally fascinated*)

BEN By God, what *is* that?

BOY 'Tis called a two-wheeled stick, Monsieur. It was just invented in Paris.

BEN (*Relishing the word as if it had never before been said*) A *Bi*-cycle! Propel it for me, would you? (*The* BOY *exits—walking it with a foot on each side. The* BOY *smiles proudly.* BEN *scowls*) Yes. Well, that could be improved. 'Tis missing something.

MAN Ah, Monsieur Franklin, are these not some of your famous inventions?

7

BEN (*Nods*) I will not deny it. I don't usually carry them around but I thought 'twould serve to advertise my cause.

WENCH (*Touching one*) The lightning rod?

BAKER'S BOY (*Pride of recognition*) The Franklin stove!

MAN (*Sits in the rocking chair and rides it wildly*) Mon dieu! An unsteady chair!

BEN (*Points at the chair*) Yes, whenever I feel lazy I get off that invention—(*Points at the chair*) and sit on this one. (*Points at the stove. Another person takes his turn in the rocker*) 'Tis called a rocking chair. If I called it "an unsteady chair" nobody'd sit in it. Same as when the British call us "a minor incident in the cold war between France and England." I much prefer The American Revolution. It's an easier chair to get King Louis to sit down in.

BENNY What was your greatest invention, Grandfather? (*The* CROWD *draws closer*)

BEN Benny . . .
    (*He lifts* BENNY *up on a crate and proceeds to over-dramatize the following fictional amusement: "I Invented Myself." He sings*)
    One dark night, a rainy one,
    Accounts for some lightning and thunder,
    For an idea, a new and a brainy one,
    I was puttering 'round, full of wonder,
    Now, what did the world really need?
    What contraption for use and for free?

8

I made a working model the following day
And I called it, "The Public Me!"
I could have called it "The Monster"
But it wouldn't have sold as well.

GIRL (*Spoken*) Tell us a little more about it.

BEN

The left hand's a poker
For stirring up trouble,
The right hand's a pipe
For blowing a bubble.
The neck is made of curtain rods
It certainly never bends.

TEMPLE (*Desperate to apologize*) My grandfather actually means . . .

BEN (*Admonishing*) Temple, see to the coach!
I invented myself out of odds and ends!
    (TEMPLE *exits*)

MAN (*Spoken*) Like a machine!

BEN Exactly! (*He sings*)
One foot is a ramrod
For ramming a door down,
One foot is a rock
For holding the floor down.
The fingers, they are feathers
Fit to tickle the other sex,
I invented myself out of bits and specks.

9

But the damn thing works,
The damn thing works,
Though it's not plumb true or level
Though it don't quite fit,
Though it ain't well knit,
The damn thing works like the devil!

The liver's a barrel
Of brandy in one sense
The lungs are two bags
Of hot air and nonsense.
I made the skin it's wrapped in
From the hide of a grizzly bear.
I invented myself out of thin blue air.

CROWD

But the damn thing works,
The damn thing works,
Though it's not plumb true or level:

BEN

Though it don't quite fit,
Though it ain't well knit,

CROWD AND BEN

The damn thing works like the devil!

CROWD

The liver's a barrel
Of brandy in one sense,
The lungs are two bags
Of hot air and nonsense.

He made the skin it's wrapped in from
The hide of a grizzly bear.

BEN
    I invented myself!

CROWD
    He invented himself!
    —Odds and ends and bits and specks,
    Fit to tickle the other sex—
    Out of thin blue air!
      (Spoken)
    The damn thing works!

TEMPLE *(Runs in)* The coach is ready, sir.

CROWD AND AMERICAN MARINES   God love you, M'sieu le
Docteur! Which way? This way, Messieurs! The way to
Paris you will know. Just follow the bells that will ring
for you—village to village! After the crowd, lads!
    (The CROWD *exits carrying the inventions)*

BENNY   May I run after the crowd, sir?

BEN   What's the good word, Benny?

BENNY   No taxation without representation!

BEN   Run after the crowd and tell them that! *(*CAPTAIN
WICKES *picks up* BENNY *in one arm,* BENNY's *suitcase in
the other, and exits)* Thank you, Captain Wickes. Keep
him in tow.

TEMPLE   I must admit, sir, I am considerable glad to find such whole-hearted love of our cause here.

BEN   Why's that?

TEMPLE   Why, if they love us here, sir, they shall recognize us right off. Why, they act as if our revolution were a show on a stage, the way they applaud it.

BEN   Yes, the hard thing will be to get 'em to pay for the ticket.

TEMPLE   Do you imply, sir, we'll have trouble getting help here?

BEN   My boy, we've got a pound of powder, an army of farmers, three uncomfortable boats and a bell with a crack in it. Would you recognize us?

TEMPLE   Then it's impossible!

BEN   Right. That's what I always have to do—the impossible.

TEMPLE   Sir? In the light of our desperate position, I beg of you to make a nice appearance in court, to wear this fine wig John Adams bought you. This excellent wig, sir.

BEN   No, sir.

TEMPLE   (*Goes right, upstage of* BEN)   You can't intend to wear that dirty beaver cap before a king!

BEN I do, sir. I want to make damn sure the King knows which one winking at him is me! Temple Franklin, cheer up. Now I don't mean to tell you what to do, but I do wish you would do what I tell you. Your father always listened to me and I made him the Governor of New Jersey. Someday you could be the Governor of Connecticut. We'll give little Benny Rhode Island.

TEMPLE Grandfather! Versailles is not like Independence Hall. 'Tis a palace. There's protocol. There's the niceties. There's social graces.

Blackout

Scene Two

The Docks transform into the Throne Room at Versailles as they speak of it.

BEN   Temple, if I were selling chandeliers, I'd wear the wig. Put it back in the box and get a grip on yourself. I was there ten years ago. Draftiest damn place you've ever been in; the court of France lives in a continual state of influenza. A warm fur cap will make me look like the only sensible man in town. Don't worry yourself, laddie, about "the monster." They may have to go some to clean me up in the history books, but—(*Puts cap on. The lights are up on a levee in progress—there is parading about, conversation*) The damn thing works!

   (*And* BEN *and* TEMPLE *step into the scene*)

COURT (*Sing daintily*)
   The "darn" thing works
   Though 'tis hardship on the ladies,
   Though it's brash or crude,
   On its head or nude
   The darn thing works like the "Hades"!

BEN
   I invented myself!

ALL
   He invented himself!

BEN
Out of thin blue . . .

ALL
Air!
He made the whole thing out of thin blue
Ha ha ha ha ha ha ha
Thin blue air!

LADY   Ah-chew!
(BEN *looks at* TEMPLE *with a "What did I tell you"*)

FOOTMAN   His Majesty, Louis the Sixteenth! King of
France.
(*Musical fanfare.* TEMPLE, COURT LADIES *and* GEN-
TLEMEN *bow.* BEN *nods, paying his respects to the
custom but not conforming.* LOUIS, VERGENNES *and*
TURGOT *enter through the center arch.* LOUIS *sits on
a small divan. Several* LADIES *kiss his hand.* LOUIS
stares at BEN *as one might stare at a Martian*)

LOUIS   Is that him? Where is Madame la Comtesse? Why
does nothing ever go right? (*A* FOOTMAN *exits*) Monsieur le Docteur, you are well known to us. Your face
is already on every snuff box in France—not to mention
how you hang in cameo down half the decolletage at this
court.
(*The* LADIES *of the court cover their bosoms with
their fans*)

BEN   I shall look into it, Your Majesty! Let me say that I
have come here as a matchmaker. I want to make a match
here between America and France. Between a young lad

of promise and a wealthy older woman. You bring us a dowry of money and guns and we shall prosper and support you later on with a good trade agreement.

LOUIS (*Nervously fingers a few notes where what he may say has been written*) As you know, Monsieur le Docteur, France loves liberty.
(TURGOT *and* VERGENNES *nod happily*)

BEN Especially in the British colonies, Your Majesty.

LOUIS (*To* VERGENNES *and* TURGOT) Why did he say that? (*They shrug—*LOUIS *finds another note*) We would do everything we could were we able to see our way clear to do anything at all.
(TURGOT *and* VERGENNES *beam.* LOUIS *squirms uncomfortably; somebody gives him an apple and he bites into it, grateful to be able to stall*)

TEMPLE (*Aside to* BEN) The British Ambassador isn't here. Let's ask for recognition now.

BEN (*Aside*) The King? . . . He isn't the one to ask.

TEMPLE (*Aside*) How do you know?

BEN (*Aside*) Look at him.

LOUIS (*To a second* FOOTMAN) Where is Madame la Comtesse? Mon dieu, I am all alone. (*The* FOOTMAN *rushes off. To* BEN) Tell me about the Indians.

BEN Why, it all began with the Indians. They had this

union of six tribes—with a system of checks and balances . . .

LOUIS (*Sees* DIANE *up center*) Thank God! There you are!

DIANE (LA COMTESSE DE VOBRILLAC) Good morning to you all! I was up all night, Louis, with that Turkish business. It's settled. There will be no war.
(*All applaud*)

LOUIS This, Monsieur le Docteur, is my very close and special friend.

TEMPLE (*To* BEN) What does he mean by that, Grandfather?

BEN I'll talk to you later.

LOUIS She is like a mother to me.

BEN (*Aside to* TEMPLE) Whoops, I'm wrong.

LOUIS (*To* BEN) Madame la Comtesse de Vobrillac.

BEN But aren't we previously acquainted, Madame?

DIANE We are, Franklin.

BEN Diane, is it?

DIANE Oui! C'est moi, cher Franklin!

BEN (*Aside*) By thunder, Temple, I know the wench.

LOUIS (*Rises and goes to* BEN) She alone was good to me when I was Dauphin, when everyone thought my grandfather would live forever and I had to steal my food from the trays being carried to the rest of them. My grandfather was a wonderful king. He could eat a raw egg. Just like a snake.

BEN Your Majesty, there is a matter I should like to discuss with you.
> (VERGENNES *and* TURGOT *move downstage to be near* LOUIS. DIANE *moves toward him.* LOUIS *looks upstage to the men, then to* DIANE, *who shakes her head, no.* LOUIS *turns back to* BEN)

LOUIS (*Sadly*) It is a pity you have not won a battle since . . . (*To* DIANE) What?

DIANE Concord Bridge.

LOUIS Oui. In our opinion, you have a lost cause. One hears your troops are reduced to fighting with bows and arrows.

BEN Of course. Superior to the gun. No smoke to cloud the aim. Quicker to load.

LOUIS He's right. Why are we using guns?

DIANE Monsieur le Docteur has come to France for guns.

BEN But I like to speak well of the bow and arrow. If my

18

words reach George the Third, he may be persuaded to issue them to the British troops.
(DIANE *nudges the King*)

LOUIS   It has been thrilling, Monsieur le Docteur, to meet the man who wrote: "Early to bed, early to rise, makes a man healthy, wealthy and wise."

BEN   Very good advice, which I've never been able to follow. (ALL *bow, curtsy and exit except* BEN, TEMPLE *and* DIANE *who chats a second to a lady of the court*) Temple, my boy, it appears that we have found the printer's devil. The one who does the dirty work.

TEMPLE   Come, Grandfather, don't even speak to her.

BEN   Nonsense. Having been turned down is simply the point at which you begin to negotiate. (*The lady of the court exits*) Temple, fetch me from the carriage the papers on the—uh—Newfoundland fishing rights.

TEMPLE   (*Proudly efficient, extends them*)   Right here, sir.

BEN   But a little diplomacy, sir, a little diplomacy. Take them to the carriage and fetch them back and dawdle along the way.

TEMPLE   But . . . Yes, sir.
(*He exits—bewildered by life*)

BEN (*To* DIANE, *referring to* TEMPLE)   Harvard. All A's.

DIANE (*Smiles*) I'm sorry, Monsieur le Docteur, for my opinion.

BEN Now, now, now! I'll hear none of that, Madame. You stick to your guns—'tis an honest opinion. I must change it for you, that's all. I can see now, that's my job in France. I was proud of you, Diane, today. Why, when first I met you ten years ago, a ragged theatre wench, you scarce could write your name! Look at you now. The grandest creature at Versailles.

DIANE Versailles to me is a continual Christmas.

BEN Oh, how you could jig and sing a Scot's air and play the hoyden in the comedies. I remember you best that weekend in Calais.

DIANE I have totally forgotten that—marvelous weekend in Calais.

BEN You wore no such fancy hairdo then—just down, plain, like silk. It's unbelievable.
        (*He sings "Too Charming"*)
    How do you do it?
    The thought of you has never ended,
    So many years, but
    I swear, Diane, I've lived suspended.

DIANE Do you feel so, Benjamin? Well, here, then, is how I feel.
        (*Sings*)
    You've always been too gallant to resist,

BEN Merci, beaucoup.

DIANE (*Sings*)
> Too gracious to conceive.

BEN   In my rude way.

DIANE (*Sings*)
> You've always been to dashing to forget

BEN   Ah!

DIANE
> And too charming to believe!
>
> Just like an iceberg
> There is more that's hidden below

BEN
> Now, that's exhilarating,
> Scintillating, stimulating, aggravating . . .

DIANE   So the answer is no!
> (*Sings*)
> You've always been too striving to restrain,
> Too stubborn to defeat.
> The mem'ry is too tender to reproach
> Yet too charming to repeat!
>
> I know you well, Ben.
> Ev'ry word, there's something behind

BEN
> Now, that's a meditating
> Fascinating, captivating, suffocating . . .

DIANE   And I won't change my mind!
> (*Sings*)
> Because you're still too gallant to resist.

BEN

> Look at that spirit!
> Look at that drive!

DIANE

> Too gracious to conceive.

BEN

> How uninviting,
> Yet how alive.

DIANE

> Too dashing to forget.

BEN

> Still intoxicating!
> Still exasperating!

DIANE

> And too winning.

BEN

> Pest'ring as a drum.

DIANE

> Too loving.

BEN

> Opposing as a thumb.

DIANE	BEN
Too gallant	Now. . . . .
Too fervent	Please. . . .
Too stubborn	Madam. . . .
Too daring	Diane. . . . .

DIANE
Too charming to believe!

BEN
Too clever to deceive!

DIANE   BEN
Too charming to believe!   Too clever to deceive!

BEN   You're proof against romance, now. You weren't, then. How could I have let ten years go by without coming to Paris!

DIANE   For someone who was the Postmaster General of North America, you could have written!

BEN   So you married a count, did you?

DIANE   Oui, Franklin.

BEN   And how is he, Madame?

DIANE   He's dead.

BEN   I'm sorry.

DIANE   No need. He was eighty-six when we married.

BEN   He died fortunate.

DIANE   And your humdrum Debby, as you called her?

BEN   Now, now, Diane, I'm a widower, too.

DIANE   Alas.

BEN Do you suppose our late mates are met in Heaven and clasped in an embrace even as we stand here?

DIANE What can we do about it, Monsieur?

BEN (*Goes to her*) Revenge ourselves on them, Madame, the first night you're free.

DIANE You rogue!

BEN We'll negotiate our differences. I'll whisper clauses to you in the dead of night. We'll spend hours in continual bargaining—this for that and that for this. But the help, the help, the help, Madame—I need that yesterday.

DIANE Do you think I am France?

BEN You counsel her king. That is France enough for me.

DIANE I won't counsel her king long if I swim against the tide. You cannot change my mind with less than a battle won against the British.

BEN (*Going toward the throne*) Whoever told you a beautiful woman should be practical?

DIANE You did. In everything you ever wrote, Franklin.

BEN (*As he casually sits on the throne without realizing it*) Didn't I ever say a person should do one foolish thing in her life for the love of another person.

DIANE (*Moving upstage*) No. That was Rousseau. (*Af-*

ter a pause) You look very good on a throne, Franklin. I hear that Congress offered you twenty thousand acres of Ohio and the assurance you'll be the first President for coming here. And it seems, therefore, to some that you are less inspired than you are salaried.

BEN   How dare you speak that way, Madame, to someone you profess to have once loved.

DIANE   You'll never get your recognition, because it is bad for France. We are not going to go bankrupt fighting Franklin's war!

BEN (*Goes to* DIANE)   I'll destroy you, Diane! You keep out of my bloody way!

DIANE   Have a care how you speak to me, Monsieur le Docteur! 'Tis one thing to have kicked your way up in a little town on the moon, but 'tis quite another matter to splash about, Monsieur, in European diplomacy in a *sophisticated* nation. (*She starts to leave*) Good day!

BEN   Good day! (*Calls after her*) No, wait.

DIANE (*She stops and waits*)   I'm waiting, M'sieu.

BEN (*He takes a pair of spectacles out of his pocket and goes to* DIANE)   Compliments of the Continental Congress—a pair of bifocals.

DIANE   Bifocals?

BEN   I invented them because I thought a man should be

25

able to see the girl in his arms at one and the same time as her husband coming in at the far door.

DIANE But there is nothing wrong with my eyesight, Monsieur.

BEN Well, you see France's problems under your nose, Madame. But what of her great advantages which lie three thousand miles away, where together we could smash the British Empire! No, Madame, your eyesight is right as rain; 'tis your insight that needs the bifocals. I'll call on you tomorrow.

(*He exits—striding off with determined pride*)

DIANE (*Sings softly*)
He's always been too pressing to deny,
Too daring to confine,
He's always been too reckless to ignore
And too charming to be mine.

(*The lights fade*)

Scene Three

In front of the blue scrim: A rattle of drums. A British Grenadier *rushes across, left to right, to the British Ambassador,* Lord Stormont, *and hands him a dispatch.*

Grenadier M'lord Ambassador, a dispatch from the war in the colonies.

Stormont (*Reads it, then cries with joy*) Excellent! A copy of this news to his Brittanic Majesty in London immediately! And a copy to the Comte de Vergennes, the Minister of Foreign Affairs at Versailles.
  (*He exits right, laughing; the* Grenadier *follows. A rattle of drums is heard. From the right and going left rushes a* French Soldier *to the French Foreign Minister,* Comte de Vergennes)

French Soldier A message from the British Embassy.

Vergennes (*Reads the dispatch*) A tragedy! Poor Franklin. I would not want to be in his breast pocket when he learns of the loss of *that* city!

SCENE FOUR

BEN FRANKLIN's *home at Passy, a suburb of Paris. It is early morning, and is still dark outside. On the wall under the staircase landing are wooden pegs holding* BENNY's *clothes. An old wooden trunk is near, a desk and a chair. A Franklin stove is set in front of the fireplace. The outside entrance to the house is through a door at the left.*

BENNY (*Coming downstairs with a heavy suitcase whistling "Yankee Doodle"*) Good morning, Cousin Temple. Is it true they wouldn't let Grandfather draft the declaration—'fraid he'd hide a dirty jest in it?

TEMPLE (*Working at the desk on ledgers and bills*) Morning, Cousin. Don't disturb me now. I'm working.

BENNY (*Looks about the dim room*) Where are you? Cannot we light a second candle, Cousin?

TEMPLE Only a few minutes to the crack of dawn, Cousin.

BENNY (*Kneels to pack some things in a trunk*) —or heat the stove? It's January. Brrrr!

TEMPLE Walk up and down! Wave your arms. That'll warm you. A penny saved is a penny earned.

28

Jerry Schaefer, Robert Preston, and Franklin Kiser,
as BENNY, BEN, and TEMPLE.

BENNY (*Takes his clothes from the pegs under the landing and packs them*) Grandfather spends money like water.

TEMPLE I know it. And you're just like him. But I'm secretary and it's me who catches it when Congress looks over these bills.

BENNY (*Sighs*) We all have our responsibilities. But tell me again, Temple, why is it I have to go to that fancy school today?

TEMPLE You have to go to that fancy school—for the thousandth time—to win friends for the cause, Benny.

BENNY Grandfather gave me a list of the ones that count.

TEMPLE Gave you a list? Sometimes he goes too far. Did he really give you a list of the ones that *count*?

BENNY (*Teasing*) Are you going to have to marry someone for the cause?

TEMPLE Marry someone for the cause? No one's said that.

BENNY (*Mischievously*) Well, we must all give our all and you have nothing else to give, do you?

TEMPLE (*Chases* BENNY *up the stairs*) You just learn your lessons, you hear. You'll grow up another Sam Adams—running around like an Indian. (BENNY *exits*) Marry someone for the cause? French diplomacy's

29

wrapped in a skirt, all right. By George, I don't think my political science professor at Harvard knew anything about diplomacy. Or else everybody else did—and only I was sitting in the dark.

(*Sings "Whatever Became of Old Temple?"*)
Oh, they'll sit around those ivy-smothered halls,
Those old men in their school ties and their shawls,
On our class reunions in the days to be,
Speaking of me.

Whatever became of old Temple?
His grandfather was a gifted man.
Well, old Temple traveled extensively in Europe
And died on the European plan.

Whatever became of old Temple?
Harvard, summer, 'seventy-six.
He never got an ounce of fun out of life.
He was one of those—you know—sticks.

I guess you could say his problem
Was he never enjoyed a misspent youth.
Even in situations
Where it was distinctly to everybody's disadvantage,
Temple told the truth.

Ruthlessly!

What the devil
Ever became of old Temple?
He must have sickened of being good.
I hear he spent quite a little time in Paris
Doing what he should
Instead of what he could.

Oh, whatever became of old Temple from school?
He grew up to become, God help me,
A loveless, respectable fool!
(*He returns to the desk and plunges back to work
in his ledger*)

BEN (*Enters down the stairs, preceded by* BENNY, *who is
carrying a footstool.* JACQUES FINQUE *helps* BEN. BENNY
takes the footstool and puts it near a love seat) Easy,
Jacques . . . Easy. Well, sir, Madame Gout has stepped
on my big toe again. Good morning, Temple.

TEMPLE Good morning, sir.

BEN (*Sits on the love seat*) Say, light another candle and
shake up the stove. You've got British weather in here.
(BENNY *pointedly grins and points at* TEMPLE. TEMPLE
chases BENNY *again—misses.* BENNY *tears up the stairs*)
We'll whup 'em, won't we, Benny?

BENNY We'll whup 'em, Grandpa.
(*He exits, followed by* JACQUES)

BEN You bet we will. We'll whup 'em.

TEMPLE (*Shakes the grate in the stove. Then rises and
lights a candle on the mantel*) Grandfather, would my
marrying well aid our cause at all?

BEN Never hurt us. Never hurt you either. A bachelor is
like half a pair of scissors. But before you marry, Temple
—where's Benny?

TEMPLE   He went upstairs.

BEN   Come here. (TEMPLE *sits near* BEN, *on the sofa*) You ever notice how a dog gets ready to lie down on a rug?

TEMPLE   Yes, sir.

BEN   Well, before a man settles down, Temple, he ought to turn about a bit . . . look around. Explore avenues.

TEMPLE   Sir?

BEN   For experience.

TEMPLE   You mean . . .

BEN   I do, sir. An older woman is preferable to a younger one.

TEMPLE   You're not serious.

BEN   I am! Why, they can educate you and keep you off the streets and in no way is the pleasure any less. For in every animal that walks upright, the body ages from the top down, you know. Leaving the lowermost plump and fetching to the last. You can take the clothes off an old woman and the clothes off a young woman, and put a basket over the head of each and I defy you to tell me which is which.

TEMPLE   (*Rises, goes downstage*)   Good God, sir. How do you know?

BEN   Hearsay. And last but not least . . . they are so grateful!

TEMPLE But if everyone were to take up with older women, sir, what would younger women do?

BEN Take up with older men, Temple. Take up with older men!

TEMPLE (*Looks out the window*) A horse!

BEN From Paris!

TEMPLE Fresh news of the war!

BEN (*Calling*) Jacques! Jacques!
    (*The front door bursts open and the author of Figaro, MONSIEUR BEAUMARCHAIS, rushes in carrying leaflets*)

BEAU Benjamin! Mon dieu!

BEN Monsieur Beaumarchais. What's the drama today, old friend? No, don't tell me. Let me guess. Figaro got married. The Barber of Seville got a haircut. No, I see it now. You've written a new play.

BEAU (*Grimly, giving a leaflet to* BEN) The British, they have taken Philadelphia.

TEMPLE God save us. Where is Congress?
    (BEN *reads to himself*)

BEAU Fled to Baltimore. Where is Baltimore? Have we a map?
    (BENNY *enters on the landing*)

33

TEMPLE   I've one in the desk.
   (*He rushes to it*)

BEAU   I was with Diane when the news arrived. Paris is desolate. She said she will never see you more. She said you were too charming and . . .

BEN   And the price just went up. Scared to death of me, is she? We've got to get at her, Beau. No French help by spring and the game is as good as . . .
   (*Notices* BENNY *on the stairs*)

TEMPLE   You were about to say, sir?

BEN (*For* BENNY'*s scared face*)   I say 'tis damned clever of Washington to have let the British take Philadelphia. Swell their heads and they'll start to make mistakes. That Washington is a military genius!

BENNY (*Coming down the steps*)   Is the war over? Is the war lost, sir?

BEN   Benny, we'll still whup 'em. Why, it's cold in Philadelphia in the winter. We'll take it back in the spring.

BEAU (*Sadly*)   With a bow and arrow. With a slingshot and a pebble. Well, what can we do—here?

BENNY (*Going to* BEN)   Goodbye, sir.

BEN   (*Absent-mindedly*)   Goodbye. (*Suddenly*) Where are you going?

34

BENNY   To that fancy school. (*Takes the list from his pocket*) I have the list.

TEMPLE   The boy's being asked too much for his age.

BEN   No, he can manage it. Turn the corners of your mouth up, Benny.

BENNY   I shall try to smile, sir.

BEN   Not good enough, sir. Now, look . . . (*Moves a foot, winces in pain*) Ouch, damned gout! Any fool can plainly see you're only *trying* to smile, Benny. If you're going to win us friends, you have to *really* smile. Why, I don't know how many times in my Almanac I wrote such good old-fashioned, but never outmoded, sentiments as:

> (*He speaks to the music, then sings "Half the Battle"*)

Half the battle
Is learning to smile,
To hold out your chest,
And lift up your chin.

Half the battle
Is picking up the pieces
And starting over again!

Half the battle's
Be true to your style,
In trouble to jest,
To toughen your skin:
Half the battle
Is rising in defiance
With the cry, I never give in!

They can think they've got me beaten,
They can knock me down,
But I'll climb up off the floor!
Just as long as I can keep alive the
Will to clown,
Well, they've won the battle
Hell, they haven't won the war!

Half the battle's
That one extra mile!
Can you meet the test?
Then, where is that grin?
With half the battle
You tuck it in your pocket
And you know then, somehow, you'll win!
   (*Spoken*)
What's the matter, Benny?

BENNY   But I have nightmares, sir. And I'm scared. Why, if they've reached Philadelphia, they've marched through New Jersey, where Uncle William is the Governor. What's happened to him? What's to become of us?

BEN   We can't bog down in questions that have no answers, lad. Now, we have to go forth in this world looking as if we hadn't a single care. Nobody lends money, laddy, to a fellow whose head is down on the buckles of his shoes. And when the French recognize us, when I walk into that throne room, Benny, and that fancy footman hollers, "The Ambassador of the United States of America!" we're going to be a country, sir. In that moment. And 'twill cost the French all their treasury to do it for us. So meanwhile, we might as well win half the battle than none at all. What do you say to that? (*Pause*)

Well, Benjamin Franklin Bache. Who are you named
after? (*Another pause*) Well?

BENNY (*Reluctantly sings*)
 Half the battle
 Is learning to smile

BEN (*Vigorously*) That's it. That's it.

BENNY
 To hold out your chest
 And lift up your chin.
  (BEN *turns to look a look at* BEAU *and winces at
  the pain in his foot*)

TEMPLE Grandfather! Your gout.
  (BEN *waves* TEMPLE *off*)

BENNY (*As the spirit rises in him*)
 Half the battle
 Is picking up the pieces
 And starting over again!

 Half the battle's
 Be true to your style,
 In trouble to jest,
 To toughen your skin:
 Half the battle
 Is rising in defiance
 With the cry, I'll never give in!

BEN AND BENNY (*Walloping loud*)
 They can think

They've got us beaten,
They can knock us down,
But we'll climb up off the floor!
Just as long as I can keep alive
The will to clown.
Well, they've won the battle . . .

BENNY

Hell, they haven't won the war!

BENNY, BEN AND TEMPLE

Half the battle's
That one extra mile!
Can you meet the test?
Then, where is that grin?
With half the battle
You tuck it in your pocket . . .

BEN (*Spoken*)   Now, let the British Embassy hear it!
      (BEAU *joins the singing*)

ALL

Half the battle
Is learning to smile,
To hold out your chest,
To lift up your chin.
Half the battle
Is rising in defiance
With the cry, I'll never give in.
You know then, somehow, you'll win.
      (JACQUES *enters*)

BEN   What is it, Jacques?

38

JACQUES Master Benny's coach is ready, M'sieu.

(He exits. TEMPLE *gets* BENNY's *suitcase.* BENNY *shakes hands with* BEN. BENNY *takes his suitcase from* TEMPLE *and starts marching off, followed by* TEMPLE *and* BEAUMARCHAIS. BEN *is left on stage alone)*

BEN *(Waving)* Goodbye, Benny. God love you. *(Goes to blow out the candles, as the day has brightened)* Oh wait, you forgot your toy balloon . . . your toy balloon! *(Holding the balloon—stops suddenly. An idea strikes him)* Of course, that's how I'll get at the wench! I could click my heels! No, I can't click my heels! Yes, I can, too, click my heels. Huzza!

(He leaps in the air, gout and all!)

Blackout

SCENE FIVE

A parade of COURT *and* RABBLE *headed toward the park—in front of a scrim.*

CRIER (*Singing*)
>A balloon is ascending
>A balloon is ascending
>A balloon is ascending
>Today.

RABBLE COUPLE
>Hooray!

CRIER
>A balloon is ascending . . .

RABBLE COUPLE
>Up is what it's intending . . .

CRIER
>On the wind it's depending . . .

ALL RABBLE
>A balloon, a balloon, a balloon.

CRIER
>A balloon is ascending . . .

ALL RABBLE
>To the moon.

CRIER
>It may.

FOUR LADIES (*Crossing*)
>Will it rise,
>And never land
>>till it's in Zanzibar?
>Will it rise
>When we have shouted
>>at it "Au revoir,"
>Or lay there—all day there?

FOOTMAN
>A balloon is arising . . .

LITTLE BOY
>Which is very surprising . . .

FOOTMAN
>Only pray we achieve it . . .

LITTLE BOY
>If I see, I'll believe it . . .

ROYALTY (*Passing*)
>More glory for France,
>More power for France,
>When flight is our exercise!

SKEPTICS (*Passing*)
>Never, never, never, never,

41

Absolutely never, never,
Never, never, never, never,
Positively never, never
Flies!

VERGENNES AND TURGOT (*Passing*)
More knowledge for France,
More honor for France.
If only the thing will rise!

MORE RABBLE
Daze our eyes,
Or will it sit as if
It's stuck in tar
And lay there?

CRIER
A balloon is ascending . . .

ALL
A balloon is ascending
A balloon is ascending
We pray!

Curtain

Scene Six

The Park. A windy day. In the foreground is a platform holding the gondola of the balloon. Three balloon attendants are holding ropes attached to the gondola.

FOOTMAN Count Pedro de Aranda, the Ambassador of Spain.
> (PEDRO *enters, followed by his* AIDE, *bows to the King and crosses*)

VERGENNES (*To* LOUIS, *who is seated center on a small blue and gold stool*) And these are the brothers Montgolfier and M'sieu Beaumarchais, Your Majesty.
> (*The Montgolfier brothers and* BEAU *enter and bow to the King*)

DIANE (*As* BEAU *joins her*) Bonjour, Beau.

BEAU Ma chère, Diane.
> (*He kisses her hand*)

DIANE You arranged all this, I understand.

BEAU In the interests of science, Madame.

DIANE Where is Franklin?

BEAU At Passy. He'll watch from his veranda.

DIANE I do not mind seeing him in public.

BEAU He heard Lord Stormont was coming, anyway.

FOOTMAN Lord Stormont, the Ambassador of Great Britain.
(STORMONT *enters, followed by a* BRITISH GRENADIER)

DIANE Monsieur Ambassador!

STORMONT (*Kisses* DIANE's *hand*) Madame la Comtesse. Now, what the dickens, Madame, do you suppose, is a big bag like that full of?

BEAU (*Looking over* STORMONT's *beefy shape*) Hot air! (STORMONT, *furious, stalks off. The balloon suddenly lifts in the wind, stops and is pulled down by the balloon attendants. The* CROWD *gasps in wonder and delight*)

PEDRO (*To* STORMONT) Back home in Spain we would have placed two criminals in such a thing. Who knows what clouds may be like? There may be pins up there.

LOUIS (*Bored, wishing to get it over with*) Let's get on with the launching. Who has the bottle? Which end is the front end?

BEAU (*To the court* PAINTER) Stand here, mon ami, so you can see!
(*He directs him to where he sets up his easel*)

DIANE (*Lifts the bottle over the gondola*)   In the name of the most glorious King Louis the Sixteenth . . .

BEAU   Excusez moi. (*To the* PAINTER) Are you recording this for posterity?

PAINTER   Oui, Monsieur.

BEAU (*As he proceeds to rearrange the "tableau" as the modern day photographer would*)   Let me see. No. Excuse me, Your Majesty. Could you move away from the gondola? And would the brothers Montgolfier come out of the gondola and stand on either side of His Majesty. I'm sorry, Madame. Excuse me. Monsieur Vergennes, over there. Pardon. Pardon. Diane, you are going to break the bottle?

DIANE   Oui.

BEAU (*Going center*)   The place for you to be is in—voilà —in the gondola itself. (*To the Montgolfier brothers*) Would you help Madame la Comtesse into the gondola? (*Both the brothers help* DIANE *into the gondola.* BEAU *walks under the ropes*) And everybody look that way, s'il vous plaît. (BEAU *slips the balloon attendant a piece of paper money*) Your Majesty, lift your chins a little. (*Pays other two balloon attendants behind his back*) Like statues! Everybody like statues! (*Looks at the* PAINTER, *who is standing like a statue*) Not you! Paint, mon ami, paint!

> (*The balloon slowly rises.* DIANE *screams. There is much confusion*)

DIANE   Help! Messieurs! Beau! Your Majesty!

PEDRO *(Lunges forward to grab a rope)*   I will save you.
        (BEAU *kicks* PEDRO. PEDRO *releases the rope. The*
        CROWD *runs off, looking up to the sky)*

BEAU *(Waving to the balloon as it goes up)*   Bon voyage!

LOUIS *(Almost in tears)*   Where is she going now?

(The lights fade)

Scene Seven

The balloon comes down into view—floating—as the clouds in the sky appear behind it. BEN *rises out of the bottom of the gondola, where he's been hidden under a robe.*

DIANE   Franklin . . . I might have known!

BEN   (*Cheerfully*) Well, I imagine, Madame, for this dark deed poor Beau won't be invited to a decent party the next six months.

DIANE   (*Eyes closed in wooziness*) I cannot concentrate on what you are saying. I am not a good sailor, Monsieur. Are we still going up?

BEN   Yes . . . and down. And up and down.

DIANE   Help! Help!

BEN   Look! There's Paris. There's Versailles. Look down.

DIANE   Never.

BEN   Why have you feared to meet me?

DIANE   I am a woman, Monsieur.

BEN (*Goes to her*) Indeed, Madame.

DIANE Stay on your side. You're tipping the balloon!
  (BEN *goes back to his side*)

BEN Let's see, by God, if we cannot steer this back to that
  weekend in Calais.

DIANE Can we steer?

BEN Montgolfier seems to think there might be some
  point in paddling. (*Gets a paddle from the bottom of
  the gondola and paddles at the air*) No, I don't think
  that does much. Where are we?

DIANE (*Relieved*) We are coming down.

BEN (*Peers over*) Quick, help me feed the stove. Pass me
  the straw!

DIANE Why?

BEN So the hot air will lift us up, Madame.

DIANE But I want to go down, Monsieur.

BEN (*Roars*) In the river, Madame?

DIANE (*With a shriek*) Oh!
  (*She quickly gives him a bundle of straw*)

BEN (*He chucks the packet into the stove*) There, that
  did it. We're a mile up, I guess.

DIANE   I think we are rocking less.

BEN   I knew it. Do you know what's happened?

DIANE   What?

BEN   Why, we have risen above our differences.

DIANE   Shame.

BEN (*Sings "To Be Alone with You"*)
How do you do it?
The wind looks wonderful in your hair.

DIANE
Stop, Monsieur Franklin—
Every scheme of yours I'm on to.

BEN
How can you rebuke me?
Just look at all the fuss I've gone to!

DIANE (*Spoken*)   You could have spared yourself the
trouble.

BEN
I'd sail the skies,
Off to the farthest little star I'd go.
Sail the skies
And watch the people disappear below.
I would gladly give up every earthly thing I know
To be alone with you.

DIANE (*Spoken*)   There you go again.

49

BEN

To be alone with you.

I'd roam the earth
And every corner of the seven seas,
Roam the earth
And face the spray of every salty breeze.
I would let the raging oceans take me where they
    please
To be alone with you.

To hold your hand in mine
With nobody here beside us.
To hold your hand in mine
There's nothing I wouldn't do.

But if some day
To have to share you with the world I must.
If some day
I find each plan of mine has turned to dust,
Then, while you're here, all that I want in all this
    world is just
To be alone with you.

DIANE

To touch the ground again
Is all that my heart can think of.
To touch the ground again
There's nothing I wouldn't do.
But while we're here
I guess I may as well forget my pride.
I'll admit
I'm awfully glad there's someone at my side.

So while we're here, I guess we might as well enjoy
   the ride
While I'm alone with you.
   (*During the orchestral interlude the balloon sails
   from one proscenium arch to the other*)

BOTH
   If some day
   To have to share you with the world I must.
   If some day
   I find each plan of mine has turned to dust
   Then, while we're here, all that I want in all this
      world is just
   To be alone with you.
   (*They embrace*)

DIANE   Ah, my dear Franklin, I wish I could help you.

BEN   You can. Get me money from the King. To buy my
guns! So I can win a battle. You said I had to win one
to change your opinion.

DIANE   You ask too much. They just took Philadelphia.

BEN   What if I get a major power to split the sum and
split the risk? Say Spain. Charles the Second and Louis
are first cousins. It'll be in the family.

DIANE   The Spanish Ambassador won't traffic with a man
who is trying to overthrow a king! How could you even
draw him into a conversation?

BEN   What do you care how I do it? I'll get to that Spanish
Ambassador through his weaknesses.

DIANE   He has none.

BEN   Then, he has one a mile wide—he's shy!

DIANE   But it is impossible!

BEN   Madame, if I cannot do the impossible, how the hell am I going to smash the British Empire?

DIANE   I might get the King to sign a memorandum on condition you involve Spain! You never will. It is giving you nothing.

BEN   You give me nothing, Madame, and I'll make something out of it.

DIANE   I want you to know I will have done it out of emotional weakness.

BEN (*So sweetly*)   Oh, Madame—no one appreciates emotional weakness more than I, for I haven't a motive in my head other than the pleasure of the moment.
    (*Sings*)
And if some day
To have to share you with the world I must.
If some day
I find each plan of mine has turned to dust,

BOTH
    Then, while we're here
    All that I want in all this world is just
    To be alone with you.
    (*The balloon rises into the sky as the lights dim*)

Scene Eight

The Pont Neuf over the Seine. A lamplighter enters and lights the lamps. A BOOKSELLER *enters, pushing his cart. A couple stroll on and cross the stage. A melancholy* TEMPLE *enters, goes to the bookstall and browses among the books. Two wenches of questionable character enter and attempt to solicit his attention. Embarrassed, he firmly declines, turning back to the bookstall. The wenches exit.*

TEMPLE   I'll take this, please. *Famous Sayings of Benjamin Franklin.*

BOOKSELLER   Fifteen sous, Monsieur.
      (JANINE, *a hot-chocolate seller, with a steaming cylinder strapped to her back, passes and eavesdrops on the conversation*)

TEMPLE (*Handing him the money*)   There you are, sir.

JANINE (*Approaching* TEMPLE)   Hot chocolate, M'sieu?

TEMPLE   No, thank you.
      (*She notices what he's bought.* TEMPLE *moves under lamp to read. She puts down her cylinder. Goes to the* BOOKSELLER)

53

JANINE   Have you another book by Benjamin Franklin?

BOOKSELLER   *Famous Sayings?*

JANINE   How much? And I am born and raised in Paris, mind you.

BOOKSELLER   I just sold the identical book for fifteen sous, but to you, ten sous.

JANINE   Two sous.

BOOKSELLER   Nine sous.

JANINE   Two sous.

BOOKSELLER   Eight.

JANINE   Two.

BOOKSELLER   Seven with a kiss. Six, I walk home with you.

JANINE   If I marry you, do I get the book for nothing?

BOOKSELLER   But I am already married, Mademoiselle.

JANINE   Shame on you. Two sous for the book.

BOOKSELLER   (*Gives her the book and takes the money from her*) You are born and raised in Paris, all right!

JANINE   How wonderful! And so cheap! Now, I kiss you for nothing.
>   (*She gives him a big kiss on the cheek. She crosses to* TEMPLE. *The* BOOKSELLER *pushes his cart off.* JANINE *thumbs through the book;* TEMPLE *gradually looks over her shoulder and realizes she has the same book*)

TEMPLE   (*Suspicious*)   Did you buy that book because I did?

JANINE   (*Casually*)   No, Monsieur.

TEMPLE   I'm sorry. I misunderstood.

JANINE   (*Reads again*)   You paid too much for it. Would you like me to make him give you your money back?

TEMPLE   No, Mademoiselle, I would not.
>   (*He goes right a few steps, then back to her*)

JANINE   (*Abruptly*)   "Fish and visitors—after three days—they stink."

TEMPLE   (*Looks back in horror*)   I beg your pardon.

JANINE   Isn't that brilliant?
>   (*She indicates a line in the book*)

TEMPLE   Oh! In the book.

JANINE   Turn to page thirty-three. "The devil wipes his nose with poor men's pride." That's my favorite saying of his. Are you married?

TEMPLE I shall never marry, Mademoiselle, unless it be to further the cause to which I am dedicated. I am an American rebel, Mademoiselle, from Boston.

JANINE *(Whispers)* I cannot marry, either. I, too, have a cause. I am a member of a newly formed French Revolution Party. *(Glances about)* Ssh!

TEMPLE *(Whispering)* How many arms do you possess? When do you strike?

JANINE Soon. We already have over twelve guns.

TEMPLE Are you training properly in the new methods?

JANINE We are training every night all over Paris.

TEMPLE Do you have ammunition?

JANINE Oh, no, Monsieur. Not yet. We are just beginning, but we are not a mob. We are not a mob.

TEMPLE How many of you are there?

JANINE Fifteen!

TEMPLE You are right. You are not a mob.

JANINE We have been in existence already four days. I am exhausted.

TEMPLE Look, revolutions take a great deal . . .

JANINE Oui, vraiment, as a matter of fact, amongst the

fifteen of us there are many factions already in serious dispute. What is your name, Monsieur?

TEMPLE (*Thrown by the abrupt question*) My name? 'Tis of no account, Mademoiselle. (*Pause*) I'm called Temple.

JANINE (*Smiling*) Temple. Janine.

TEMPLE Janine.

JANINE You have never been in love, have you, Temple?

TEMPLE (*Stiffly*) Correct. It evidently shows. Everybody assumes it.

JANINE Me neither. I am really very shy.

TEMPLE (*Very matter-of-factly*) One would never know it.

JANINE Well, shy for a Parisienne, I mean. But you, I'll wager, pass for shy in Boston, but no matter—you're in Paris now. And—
  (*Sings "You're in Paris"*)
If you're shy, Paris will make you bold.
If you're naïve, Paris will see you're told.
If you're old, Paris will make you young.
That is a Paris art;
To teach you a foreign tongue to talk,
Heart to heart.

You're in Paris, you're in Paris,
You're in Paris, where the fashion is romance.
If you listen, dare to listen,
Soon your heart will start to dance
To the music that is Paris.

You're in Paris, that's where you are:
Dreams come true are just a part of her
Design.
'Neath a garret's rafter
There's more laughter
In the Paris wine,

Street cafés of an evening fill up two
By two,
Dawn by the river's good for strolling through:
Wouldn't you love
To be in love
In Paris?
You're in Paris!

CHORUS (*Seen through the Pont Neuf scrim*)
You're in Paris, you're in Paris,
You're in Paris, where the fashion is romance.
If you listen, dare to listen,
Soon your heart will start to dance
To the music that is Paris.

You're in Paris, that's where you are:
Dreams come true are just a part of her
Design.

'Neath a garret's rafter
There's more laughter
In the Paris wine,
Street cafés of an evening fill up two
By two,
Dawn by the river's good for strolling through:
Wouldn't you love
To be in love
In Paris?

Curtain

Scene Nine

*Paristown. Two tables with chairs are before a café. The
street is crowded. A ballet takes place in which the rabble
army reveal themselves to be about as clumsy and inept as
one could imagine—*TEMPLE *takes over and shows them
how to fight from behind trees, etc. He rapidly turns them
into a crack precision marvel. The dance ends.* JANINE
glows with pride.

JACQUES (*Entering*) Excuse me, Mademoiselle. (*Then
to* TEMPLE) Monsieur *Franklin?* (TEMPLE *tries to shush*
JACQUES, *but* JANINE *has heard the name*) Your grandfather left a coach at your disposal. Are you ready to go
back to Passy now, Monsieur?

JANINE (*Very slowly*) Are you the grandson of Benjamin Franklin?

TEMPLE Unfortunately, Mademoiselle.

JANINE (*Gloriously*) But you are a wonderful person for
you to be! Imagine, to be such an interesting man *and*
the grandson, too!

TEMPLE Did you find me "interesting," Mademoiselle?

JANINE More interesting than reading his book. (*She*

60

tosses it away. Someone catches it—exits reading) There! And it cost me money, too.

TEMPLE (*With impulsive decision*) Jacques, we're not going to Passy. We're going anywhere Mademoiselle desires as long as anywhere we go, we're in Paris.

JACQUES Oui, Monsieur.
  (*He smiles and exits*)

CHORUS
  'Neath a garret's rafter
  There's more laughter
  In the Paris wine.

JANINE And you must give your book back too, or I won't go—as a gesture of—independence!

TEMPLE Mademoiselle, you have a point.
  (*He hurls the book offstage and sings*)
  I'm in Paris!
  (*JANINE takes his hand, they walk off, staring at one another*)

CHORUS (*With a knowingness*)
  You're in Paris . . .
  You're in Paris.

    (*The lights fade as all drift away*)

Scene Ten

BEN FRANKLIN's *house at Passy.* BEN *is alone on stage holding a memo from* LOUIS—*in preparation to departing for an appointment.*

BEN (*Calls off*) Jacques! Where's that traveling desk I invented? Invent a portable desk and you never can find it. Serves me right.
> (BEAU *enters from upstairs carrying the traveling desk*)

BEAU Jacques is readying the coach. I have the traveling desk. Where's Temple? Is he going with us?

BEN (*Sits on the love seat*) Temple rode into Paris to "distribute leaflets."

BEAU Again leaflets?

BEN That's what he calls it, bless him. I trust 'tis an older woman.
> (BEN *takes the traveling desk and checks inside it for the quill pens*)

BEAU Will you do me a favor? Will you unveil this plot? Why are we taking a traveling desk to a monastery?

BEN Diane's help from King Louis wants matching. We may get the Spanish Ambassador in a signing mood to-day.

BEAU Something tells me, that Spanish Ambassador, he does not like us.

BEN What tells you that?

BEAU The last three times his footman slammed the door in our faces made me suspicious.

BEN We'll win him over. We must. Washington writes that he can hold out only three months more.

BEAU Benjamin . . . I . . .

BEN No, Beau.

BEAU How do you know what I was going to say?

BEN You say it every day.

BEAU Then, I will say it again. Please, Benjamin . . . give me a passport to America. Let me follow Lafayette. Let me fight with Washington! Oh, to whack my way through the wilderness!

BEN You'll rip your velvet britches on a picket fence!
(*He puts the quill pens back in the desk*)

BEAU Feel my muscle—feel it!

BEN   That's your writing arm, Beau.

BEAU   The war for liberty is over there!

BEN   No, it is here. This is where the guns are!

BEAU   Practical, always practical. (*Goes near the table*) Did you never write that a man should die for liberty?

BEN   No. (*He rises and takes the desk to* BEAU) I wrote, "A fox must wake up and trot for a chicken in the pot." Go yell a "vite, vite" at Jacques, will you, please?

BEAU   (*Goes to door, carrying the traveling desk*)   Alas, Benjamin, have you never suffered from idealism?

BEN   I should like to have, Beau, but I haven't found an awful lot of time to indulge in it. (BEAU *exits.* BEN, *to himself*) Yes . . . a cat must take off his gloves to catch those mice he loves. And we're none of us saints, Beau, we're none of us saints! (*He starts up the stairs. There is a knock at the door*) Turn the little knob, my friend. (DIANE *enters.* BEN, *in surprise*) Madame!

DIANE   (*Beaming*)   Voilà! I brought the plans. (*Goes to the desk*) Come. You must look and approve.

BEN   What plans?

BEAU   (*From offstage*)   Benjamin, the coach is ready!

BEN   At once! (*To* DIANE) You should have sent me word that you meant to trot in on me today. I'm off to hunt down my Spanish Ambassador. What are you clutching there?

DIANE (*Holding up a rolled-up blueprint*) Your laboratory. The one you agreed to let me build for you in my house.

BEN Well, we'll snatch a moment for that. You shouldn't have, but since you did. (*Opens a door and calls*) One moment, Beau! (*Closes the door.* DIANE *unrolls the blueprint on the desk.* BEN *goes to it*) You know what I most ache to do these days is to propose . . .

DIANE Oui?

BEN . . . scientific questions that no one knows the answers to.

DIANE Oh.

BEN And I've been dreaming of late . . .

DIANE Oui?

BEN . . . about some oyster shells I found in the Adirondacks once.

DIANE (*Drily*) Really, Franklin?

BEN It makes me think those mountains may once have been the ocean floor. I mean it would be fun to prove that, wouldn't it?

DIANE   The most curious things amuse you sometimes.

BEN   What's all this? Here on the plans.

DIANE   This? This is your sitting room.

BEN   My sitting room. This?

DIANE   (*Points with her finger*)   Library. Bedchamber. Kitchen.

BEN   I see. This is something more than "a little laboratory," Madame. Did you intend me to reside with you entirely?

DIANE   It just grew. I thought, whatever will he do should he desire to eat; and then, and what if he gets sleepy; and then, and suppose he needs a book, or many books?

BEN   And this?

DIANE   (*Weakly*)   An indoor tennis court.

BEN   (*Sharply*)   For me? For what?

DIANE   For play. One has to play.

BEN   Why can't I play at my house?

BEAU   (*From offstage*)   Benjamin! Washington has only three months!

BEN   (*Calling to him*)   I'm coming!

66

DIANE You grow cross, Monsieur?

BEN (*Rolls up the blueprint*) Well, Madame, I smell a rat.

DIANE A rat?

BEN (*Gives the plans to* DIANE) And his name is matrimony.

DIANE How dare you!

BEN No? We spoke of a few glass tubes in a temporary corner!
    (BEN *puts on his coat*)

DIANE You said when the war is over, you could be nowhere as well cared for as here.

BEN But I didn't say I intended to devote my life to being well cared for, did I?

DIANE No, but you let me assume you did.

BEN Do you adore me, Madame?

DIANE Not every day, Monsieur.

BEN Well, invest the architect's fees in the Continental Army if you adore me.

DIANE That day in the balloon . . .

BEN I never made a statement.

DIANE You insinuated, you implied, and you hinted.

BEN But I never made a statement. I know I didn't be-cause I took great pains not to, and it wasn't easy.
    (*He picks up his cane*)

DIANE Do you adore *me*, Monsieur?

BEN (*Pause*) But I have a job to do and I don't have for-ever to do it in.

BEAU (*From offstage*) Benjamin!

BEN (*Going to the door*) Coming!

DIANE You'll never get your Spanish Ambassador unless you can perform miracles.

BEN (*Stops*) I'll get him. And I'll win a battle. And France will recognize us! It will happen.

DIANE Then, you no longer have any need of me, Monsieur.

BEN Madame, you live in a poem and I live in a news-paper's bold type where the ink's still wet on the page.

DIANE You are obsessed with posterity, Monsieur. 'Tis unmanly.

BEN And you are drunk with power, Madame. 'Tis un-feminine. Good afternoon.
    (*He exits*)

DIANE (*Stonily*)   Good afternoon . . . (*Her bravery then
dissolves. She runs to the door*) Benjamin!
   (*But the sound of horses galloping off stops her.
   Sings "How Laughable It Is"*)
Ah, how laughable it is
That you always adore
The very one you never
Can live with.

And how laughable it is
When your love's not returned.
You face a fact and that's what
You live with, in a lifetime.

What a joke on people
Is human feeling,
That lets them thrill
Before the kill
That leaves them reeling.

How laughable it is
That my heart runs to hug
The very love that never
Can ever be.

I have everything my life requires
Except the thing my heart desires,
Someone who can make me dependent and free.
Laughable it is
And the laugh is on me.

Blackout

Scene Eleven

The merry MONKS *of Morellet carry bunches of grapes in procession across the stage.*

MONKS (*Three* MONKS *enter, singing* "Hic Haec Hoc")
>   Hic haec hoc
>   In vino veritas
>   Hic haec hoc,
>   Hic haec hoc.
>
>   Hic haec hoc,
>   In vino veritas,
>   Hic haec hoc,
>   Hic haec hoc!
>
>   (*Three more* MONKS *enter*)
>   Hic haec hoc
>   In vino veritas
>   Hic haec hoc,
>   Hic haec hoc.
>
>   Hic haec hoc
>   In vino veritas,
>   Hic haec hoc,
>   Hic haec hoc!
>
>   (*Three additional* MONKS *enter*)
>   Sic semper tyrannus,

Semper fidelus,
In vino veritas,
Hic haec hoc.
Sic semper tyrannus,
Semper paratas,
In vino veritas,
Hic haec hoc!

(*The last group of three enter*)
Hic haec hoc
In vino veritas
Hic haec hoc,
Hic haec hoc.

Hic haec hoc,
In vino veritas,
Hic haec hoc.

In vino veritas
In vino veritas
In vino veritas
In vino veritas
Hic . . .
   (*They run upstage*)
Haec hoc!

Blackout

Scene Twelve

The winery at the Abbey de Morellet. An afternoon in April. A wooden bench, huge wooden vat and a large barrel are on stage. In the background, seen through the arches of a shed, are the vineyards. Empty grape baskets are lined up all the way across the stage near the vat.

ABBÉ To thy work, brothers. (*The* MONKS *pick up their baskets and exit. The* SPANISH AMBASSADOR, *followed by his* AIDE, *enter. The* ABBÉ *crosses to him*) Mon cher Ambassador, you are about to witness the treading of the grape.
  (*He throws his bunch of grapes into the vat, in a careless fashion*)

PEDRO (*Deadly serious*) A slippery business, mon cher Abbé.
  (*He takes off his hat and gives it to his* AIDE)

BEAU (*Entering, followed by* BEN) Monsieur l'Abbé, am I too late for the grape? I brought Monsieur le Docteur.
  (PEDRO *snatches his hat again*)

PEDRO (*Turns to go*) Nonsense! It is a trick!

BEN A trick on me. Beau, we leave at once.

PEDRO *I* am leaving.

BEN *I* am leaving. *You* can stay.

PEDRO (*Begins to leave*) No, I should leave. You are the one who plotted the encounter.

BEN Then, why should I be leaving?

PEDRO Well, I . . .

BEN What do you want, sir?

PEDRO I don't want anything. (*Goes toward* BEN) You want a piece of paper to match the piece of paper Louis gave you. You need half the money from me, right?

BEN Congratulations on your espionage system.

PEDRO Gracias.

BEN He's the best cook I ever had, too. But he's about two weeks behind the news. I no longer have any need of Spain.
    (*He starts out.* BEAU *follows*)

PEDRO Wait! (BEN *and* BEAU *back up two steps and await the taking of the bait*) Is it Holland? Is it Russia? Did they give you the money?

BEN It is too late, Señor, for politics. I am sorry I cannot have one tiny drink with you, but I have determined to

73

BEN FRANKLIN IN PARIS

abstain from strong spirits till the war is won. (*Turns to* BEAU) I find my tongue loosens and I tell all.
(*A* MONK *carrying a tray with glasses enters*)

PEDRO (*Getting the idea as a glass is handed to him*)   Let us have a tiny drink together.

BEN   No, no. Unless a toast is called for by an official diplomat, I cannot.

PEDRO   Then, I propose a toast. I'm an official diplomat.

BEN   Please don't. I must go. We'll only get into that silly business where you make a toast and I, due to protocol, will have to respond with a toast. I have no time for that.
(BEN *and* BEAU *start off*)

PEDRO   A toast! Let me see.

BEAU (*Whispers to* PEDRO *as he passes him*)   Concord Bridge. Bunker Hill.

PEDRO   To the Bridge of Concord!

BEN   Damn! (*Mock pretense of being caught. He returns and raises a glass*) To the bridge!
(*They drink, put the empty glasses back on the tray*)

PEDRO (*Taking a second glass from the tray—slyly*)   To the Hill of Bunker!

BEN (*Taking a second glass*)   Wait your turn! To Don Quixote!

PEDRO (*With passion*) To Don Quixote!
(*They drink*)

ABBÉ (*To* PEDRO—*rubbing it in*) But I thought you didn't want to meet him.

PEDRO (*To the* ABBÉ) Shhhhh! (*Turns to* BEN. *Each takes new drinks*) Now, to the Hill of Bunker!

BEN And that's the end of it. Bunker Hill! (*They drink and put their glasses back on the tray*) You make fine Spanish lace in your country, Señor, but where I come from we accomplish the same effect by simply not mending our clothes—in time, it becomes lace.

PEDRO Ingenious. You have not yet responded to my second toast, sir.
(*A second* MONK *enters carrying a tray of drinks*)

BEN (*Taking a drink; all follow*) As we say in America, to the wool over your eyes!

PEDRO (*Oblivious*) To the wool over my eyes!
(*They drink. Other* MONKS *enter*)

BEAU (*To the* ABBÉ) Magnificent wine, Monsieur Abbé. How ever did you achieve the flavor?

MONK (*Answering for the* ABBÉ) Some of the cows got into the—

ABBÉ (*Quickly*) Messieurs, I give you the blessings of God.

75

ALL To the blessings of God!
     (*All drink*)

BEN And now, Señor, I *must* go.

PEDRO But we cannot stop now. We must, tralala, have
another toast.

BEAU To what?

PEDRO To what? To . . . to . . . (*Sadly*) There is nothing left to toast.

BEN I know one. Here's to what we all adore—

PEDRO I beg of you, Monsieur, remember where we are.

BEN Ah, yes, well—gentlemen, I give you the elbow.

PEDRO The elbow?

BEN (*To all*)
     A neglected annex of the arm,
     A practical piece of poetry, sirs.
     A tough hide covering a thing of lovely
     Flexibility.

     That flowers should grow is no wonder at all
     For the seed and the soil make it obvious
     To any.

     But that there should flourish
     Between the shoulders and the wrists

76

Robert Preston and Ulla Sallert as BEN and DIANE.

That surprising joint of joints
Is a matter for philosophers to ponder.

For, gentlemen, when all is said and done,
What is it, after all, with which one tests
A baby's bath?

(*Sings "God Bless the Human Elbow"*)
God bless the human elbow,
God bless it where it bends.
If it bent too long,
We'd be dry I fear;
If it bent too short,
We'd be drinking through our ear,
But
It bends just right,
In the middle of the arm,
Not too loose, not too tight,
As we lean on it each night,
With a well-oiled kind of charm,

BEN, BEAU AND PEDRO

With a well-oiled kind of charm!

BEN

When the brain won't tick,
When the heart won't leap,
When the stomach feels sick,
When the foot's asleep,
Then, we point man and boy,

BOTH

As its wonders we employ
To that luckily knuckling, anatomical joy.

77

ALL
>God bless the human elbow,
>God bless it where it bends.
>If it bent too long,
>We'd be dry I fear;
>If it bent too short,
>We'd be drinking through our ear,
>But
>It bends just right,
>In the middle of the arm,
>Not too loose, not too tight,
>As we lean on it each night,
>With a well-oiled kind of charm,
>With a well-oiled kind of charm!

MONKS (*Sing as they exit right and left*)
>Hic haec hoc
>In vino veritas,
>Hic haec hoc
>Hic haec hoc . . .

PEDRO   Is it Holland? John Adams got it in Amsterdam —true or false!

BEN   And to think, sir, you tried to slam the door in my face.

PEDRO   I didn't realize. All I know is what's good enough for Holland is good enough for us.

BEN   Well, I haven't signed yet.

PEDRO   Wonderful! Don't sign!
(*Offstage we hear the* MONKS *singing*)

MONKS

Hic haec hoc
In vino veritas,
Hic haec hoc
Hic haec hoc.

BEN

I'll think about it! Meanwhile,
enjoy yourself, Pedro.

PEDRO

Ha ha! I am enjoying myself!

(*The* MONKS *enter left and right carrying baskets of grapes—on the run*)

Hic haec hoc
In vino veritas,
Hic haec hoc
Hic haec hoc.

BEN

Come, Beau, unbuckle your shoes
and let us tread the grapes!

(BEN *and* BEAU *take off their shoes, go up center and jump into the vat*)

PEDRO   Gentlemen, make way for a matador!

(*Caught up in the spirit,* PEDRO *strides toward the vat as if in the bull ring*)

MONKS

God bless the human elbow,
God bless it where it bends.
If it bent too long,
We'd be dry I fear;
If it bent too short,
We'd be drinking through our
    ear . . .

MONKS

Hic haec hoc
In vino veritas,
Hic haec hoc
Hic haec hoc.

Hic haec hoc
In vino veritas,
Hic haec hoc
Hic haec hoc.

PEDRO (*To* BEN) Am I in? Am I in?

BEN (*Debating*) Well?

PEDRO I give you my word as a gentleman. Spain's money is pledged.

BEN The business is done.
(*They shake hands.* BEAU *gets the traveling desk from behind the vat*)

PEDRO Sí. And I have given it to you!

BEN No, Pedro, I have given it to you!

PEDRO And I have loved every minute of it!
(*He signs the paper*)

ALL
God bless the human elbow,
God bless it where it bends.
If it bent too long,
We'd be dry I fear;
If it bent too short,
We'd be drinking through our ear . . .
(*The sky has gotten darker. Flashes of lightning and thunder send the* MONKS *scurrying, leaving* BEAU *and* BEN *with their shoes in their hands, and the precious paper held aloft as the lights go out*)

BEN (*As the lights go up, it is later that night.* BEAU *and* BEN *are a little worse for the long night's drinking*)
What a night! God bless that Spaniard's elbow! And his wrist, too.

BEAU   If you sit down, my dear Benjamin, we can never get to where we're going.
(*Lightning*)

BEN   Where I was going was to sit down. (*Sits on wheelbarrow. Soft thunder*) What a night! In vino veritas. In wine, sir, there is truth. And the truth is, Beau, (*Then feelingly*) last July, we got pregnant. And the day we get recognition we'll be born on that day. But tonight— Sit down, Beau, before you fall down—(BEAU *sits to the left of* BEN) tonight, we felt life. Money and guns. Life! A stirring in the belly of the war. Liberty is alive! (*A zigzag of lightning cuts across the sky followed by loud thunder. The two men look at it*) I caught some of that once!

BEAU   Huh? Ah, oui!

BEN   I touched it, Beau, with my naked finger and I felt it across the blades of my back. Now, I believe I have it in my fingers—residual—in the palm of my hand.

BEAU   Is this a scientific opinion?

BEN   Spiritual. In keeping with a monastic occasion.

BEAU   I thought you were an atheist.

BEN   Agnostic.

BEAU   What difference?

BEN   Every. An atheist is happy there's no God. An agnostic feels lonely about it. Have it in my brain somehow—that fire from the old Greek gods will not let me rest as long as I live.

(*Lightning is followed by soft thunder*)

BEAU (*Rises*)   I think you are in love. Do not deny it.

BEN   Yes, I am in love!

BEAU   With Diane de Vobrillac!

BEN (*Rises*)   Are you mad? The love of a woman? Does a whirlwind love a woman? (*Lightning. Loud thunder*) I'm in love with electricity! I'm in love with necessity! (*Lightning*) I am a forest in flames and you want to know if I have stolen any kisses lately.

BEAU   I still think you love her.

BEN   That's because you're a playwright. And a popular playwright. You'd think a tree loved a rock if you could get five acts out of it.

BEAU   Agnostic!

ABBÉ (*Calling from offstage*)   Holla, Monsieur . . .

BEAU   'Tis the Abbé. He has the carriage. Here! Here! This way!

(*Lightning. Soft thunder.* BEAU *exits*)

BEN (*Kneels and looks up*)   Well, God, sir . . . (*The thunder answers him gently—*BEN *nods back*) as one agnostic to another, let me put it to you, sir, as from one who is scarce a gentleman, but half a scholar and an eager skeptic—is it wrong to refuse to love someone—someone you love? Or does that mean, you may love something more. I don't know what. When I invented myself, I left out—a heart, perhaps. Oh, yes. And— Is it wrong to want to make men free—and also to want twenty thousand acres of Ohio territory and to be President.

(*Thunder*)

BEAU (*Calling from offstage*) Benjamin! (*Enters, carrying* BEN's *cape*) What are you doing? The Abbé has the carriage. What did you lose?

BEN (*Rising*) My confidence, but only for the merest moment. (BEAU *helps* BEN *put on his cape*) Come, Beau, let's get to purchasing those guns and shipping them to where they can be useful!

BEAU Oui! Come, my friend.
(*He exits*)

BEN Lost my confidence? What's happening to me? Well, 'tis of no great consequence. I'm the man I always was! The damn thing works!
(*Sings*)
Though it don't quite fit,
Though it ain't well knit,
The damn thing works like the devil!
(*Lightning, loud thunder.* BEN *strides off*)

Curtain

Act Two

Scene One

The garden of the Spanish Embassy in Paris. An early, velvet, pleasant evening in 1777. Dancers are seen through the windows of the terrace. A SPANISH SOLDIER *stands on watch.* JANINE *enters and runs up to the arches to watch the dancing.*

SOLDIER   Halt! Who goes there?

JANINE *(Ducks in the shadows)*   Emissary to the Spanish Ambassador, resume your watch!

SOLDIER *(Reaches to her and pulls her out)*   Just a moment. Step into the light first.

JANINE   But all I want is to peer in at the dancing.

SOLDIER   No, you don't.

JANINE   But my lover, my lover is in there.

SOLDIER   Which one?
      *(*TEMPLE *and the* SPANISH AMBASSADOR'S DAUGHTER *dance out on the terrace)*

JANINE   There. That one dancing with the tall wench.

87

SOLDIER   With the Spanish Ambassador's daughter?

JANINE   Oui. I know that. He has to dance with her—it is part of his job. You see, he is a diplomat.

SOLDIER   Sí. I believe he is. (*Laughs*) All right, wench. Peer in at your betters if it makes you happy. Or you might go round to the kitchen and dance with the servant lads if you'd like.

JANINE   No, merci. I would only dance with the person I love.

SOLDIER   And no one else?

JANINE   Not unless he be—Benjamin Franklin!

SOLDIER   Ah, there's a faithless wench in Madrid I would had your philosophy!
(*He exits*)

JANINE (*Hums and moves, alone; then, sings to herself "When I Dance with the Person I Love"*)
I melt like butter in the sunshine,
Reflect like candlelight and wine,
Out loud. I hum,
In delirium,
When I dance with the person I love!

As limp as linen on a handloom,
I fly, a witch without a broom,
My heart, down deep,
Does a dolphin-leap,
When I dance with the person I love!

And, oh, if he ever should go away,
I'd be true,
True, I'd stay,
Waiting the rest of my life till he
Could renew the dance with me!

In what way better, could I spend time,
I climb where ladders cannot climb,
I float o'er town
Made of eiderdown,
Oh, it tenders me, gentles me, sets me above,
When I dance with the person I love!
  (BEN *comes onto the terrace.* JANINE *bumps into him*)

BEN (*Amused*) Good evening.

JANINE (*Numb—then, rallying*) Good evening. You do not know me, Monsieur le Docteur, but one day you will know me very well.

BEN I hope I shall. May I have what name to call you by?

JANINE No. A nameless girl you met one night in the garden of the Spanish Embassy in Paris.

BEN There speaks a romantic spirit.

JANINE With a militant side as well. (*A step to* BEN) How goes the war?

BEN I wait good news by the second.

JANINE One hears you've acquired guns.

BEN   We have.

JANINE   I have twelve guns I would very much like to offer. (*Pause*) We were premature.

BEN   I'll pay you for them.

JANINE   No. They are not such good guns, but they are something. When a mysterious box of twelve guns arrives at Passy, you will know I have kept my word.

BEN   Thank you. Won't you be my guest and come inside and I'll find you a proper partner with whom to dance?

JANINE   (*Boldly*)   The more fool me to say yes; here, I have you all to myself.

BEN   Oh, you've a winning way, my nameless friend. I wonder how *you'd* go about winning France to an alliance with America?

JANINE   I would tell them—"Messieurs, France should dance with the person she loves, for if a nation, like an older woman, like myself, in fact, were to say, 'I will not dance but with the person I love,' then she would be happy in that singular alliance, for 'twould be more marriage than contract."

BEN   (*Nodding, charmed by the thoughtful truth*)   And more heart than head. 'Tis a difficult choice, that of one's own true love.

JANINE (*A step toward* BEN)   No, 'tis easy, for I think if we lost the war in which we were allied 'twould destroy us here. So one chooses one's true love by saying to one-self: "For this true love, I would gamble with my life—and nothing less!"

BEN   Just for that, would "an older woman" be inclined to dance with a man to whom she is a younger woman.

JANINE   You are not my true love, Monsieur le Docteur, but you are—the exception to the rule.
(*They dance and are joined by the other couples*)

BEN (*Taking her hand and pulling her toward the center arch*)   Come here. I want your opinion on something.

JANINE   Gladly.

BEN   There. That lad with the tall wench?

JANINE   Oui.

BEN   He's my grandson.

JANINE (*Proudly*) Oui.

BEN   Well, what do you think?

JANINE   Of him?

BEN   Of them. Of them. That tall wench and him. 'Tis a good match, I think. A good alliance. I did the same for my son, Bill, his father. Prospered him all the way to the

Governorship of New Jersey. Now, you've a wise heart, have I done well by him or not? She's the daughter of a count, this one.

JANINE (*Softly*) You are the son of a candlestick-maker.

BEN (*Unaware of her feelings and pleased*) Right. That's a long way to have come in two generations.

JANINE Oui. 'Tis a long way. I wish him and you all the good fortune in the world.
(*Bells are heard ringing in the distance—the people pour out into the garden*)

PEDRO (*Enters, to* BEN) Monsieur le Docteur . . .
(BEN *turns. An American* MARINE *enters and hands* BEN *a dispatch.* BEN *reads it to himself*)

BEN (*Looking up; and then softly, in excitement*) Saratoga. We've won a battle at Saratoga. We took an entire British army at Saratoga! With the guns! With the guns!
(*All cluster around him and congratulate him*)

BEAU (*Entering*) The coach has been brought around. I thought you'd want to drive directly to Versailles.

BEN Good, Beau. Good. She'll see it now. Lost cause, is it? I want recognition. I want it *now!* Yes, sir.
(*He goes into the house and exits, the people following him.* TEMPLE *and the* SPANISH AMBASSADOR'S DAUGHTER *are left on stage.* TEMPLE *sees* JANINE)

TEMPLE Janine!

JANINE (*Trembling*)   Bonne chance, Monsieur Franklin! Vive la victoire!
 (*She runs off*)

AMBASSADOR'S DAUGHTER   Señor! Will you not go with me?

TEMPLE (*Looks after* JANINE, *then turns to the* AMBASSADOR'S DAUGHTER. *With an overtone of irony, choosing* BEN's *pragmatism*)   The best offer of the evening, Señorita . . . is the expedient thing to do.

 (*They go inside as the lights fade*)

Scene Two

A corridor at Versailles. BEN, TEMPLE *and* BEAU *come on from one side, and the British Ambassador,* DAVID LORD STORMONT *enters from the other. They meet center stage.*

BEN (*Knowing him from London days in the past*) Davy, (*They shake hands*)

STORMONT (*With guarded politesse*) Ben.

BEN You know Monsieur Beaumarchais.

STORMONT We've met at the plays.

BEN My grandson. This is David Lord Stormont, the British Ambassador, Temple. (STORMONT *offers his hand.* TEMPLE *nods stiffly.* BEN *smiles and turns to* STORMONT) Shaking hands with the enemy comes hard to him.

STORMONT Politics is an old man's checkers. You're on your way to the Throne Room, sir.

BEN We are, sir.

STORMONT Congratulations on this Saratoga business.

94

BEN   Thank you, Davy. Now, if you'll excuse us, we're in a bloody hurry.

(BEN, TEMPLE *and* BEAU *go past* STORMONT *and start to exit*)

STORMONT   No doubt you are. But don't look for recognition, Ben. (BEN *turns and faces him*) You're not going to get it.

BEN   They know we can beat you now.

STORMONT   Not with the population in the colonies rapidly turning to us.

BEN (*Sensing* STORMONT *knows something*)   What do you mean?

TEMPLE   Tory bluff, Grandfather.

BEN   No, Temple, no.

STORMONT   Your son, Ben.

BEN   What of him, sir?

STORMONT (*To* TEMPLE)   And your father, lad. Your son and your father, gentlemen, the Honorable William Franklin, the Governor of New Jersey, has come over to us and fights the American rebels in the field today!

TEMPLE   Then he's a traitor, sir!

STORMONT   A traitor to traitors is a loyalist, sir. Naturally

95

I have every written proof of this and have submitted it to the Court of France. Gentlemen, this jig is at an end. You may have won a battle, but you can't win the war without a French Alliance. Washington's in Valley Forge at the moment, lots of glory and no food. Ben, come with me to London now and let's draw up a treaty of peace and stop the war!

BEN Without independence?

STORMONT Beggars can't be choosers.

BEN David, it's a bit much to have one's own aphorism quoted back at one. David, I'll tell you truly, what I would like to do to you, I would you could do to yourself, sir.

STORMONT (*Coloring*) Ben, you're a fool!

BEN What's wise about going to London? Once you got me there you'd hang me.

STORMONT Your personal safety would be guaranteed by King George the Third.

BEN Oh, that's a comfort, Davy.

STORMONT I shall be available to you, night and day. If you change your mind. (STORMONT *starts away, but turns*) And I must tell you, sir, I didn't expect you to break down and weep before *me* on hearing what must be tragic news for a father, but I did expect the *faintest human reaction*.

BEN (*Measuredly*) I'd rather he hadn't done it. On the other hand, 'tis the first time in his life he ever showed a little spine.

STORMONT   You, sir, are an incomprehensible creature. (*He exits*)

TEMPLE   You don't mean that, sir.

BEN   I absolutely do, sir.

TEMPLE   But you did everything for him.

BEN   Because he let me. (*And then*) You don't love that Spanish girl a bit.

TEMPLE   True!

BEN   Then, what the hell are you marrying her for?

TEMPLE   Because you told me to.

BEN   Then tell me to go to hell! You love another girl?

TEMPLE   Yes, sir.

BEN   French girl?

TEMPLE   Yes, sir.

BEN   Poor girl?

TEMPLE   Yes, sir.

BEN Nice girl?

TEMPLE Yes, sir.

BEN Do you care if you never become Governor of Connecticut?

TEMPLE No, sir.

BEN What do you look for in life?

TEMPLE Small pleasures, sir.

BEN And what do you have to say to me?

TEMPLE (*Pause*) Go to hell, sir.

BEN (*Softly*) Go to her, sir. (TEMPLE *goes*) And bring her home with you so I can meet her.

TEMPLE Yes, *sir!*
  (*He exits*)

BEAU All is lost! The war is lost!

BEN God, you give up easy!

BEAU But it's impossible!

BEN Of course it is, but that's what I always have to do . . . the impossible!
  (BEN *strides off, followed by* BEAU)

Curtain

SCENE THREE

DIANE's *morning room in her chateau, on an island in the Seine. A double door is at the right. A small table with a mirror and flowers is upstage of the door. In the center of the room is a love seat. On the left wall is a fireplace —on each side of the fireplace is a small table with flowers. Downstage of the fireplace is an upholstered stool.* TURGOT *stands near the fireplace with pad and pen in hand.*

DIANE (*Pacing below the sofa, carrying a page of notes*) Suggestion . . . to transfer the second army to the Swiss border for maneuvers. Suggestion . . . to cut by half the tax in District Thirteen. They can't afford it. Suggestion to His Majesty . . . that he is to take a bath on Tuesday —with soap. (YVONNE *enters*) What is it, Yvonne? Can't you see I'm extremely busy.

YVONNE   But he pushed past the footman.

DIANE   Who pushed past the . . . ? Why do I ask?

YVONNE   Monsieur le Docteur.

DIANE (*She dismisses the man with a wave of her hand*) After four months' silence—how dare he?

YVONNE   With a gift for Madame.

99

DIANE What else? I can't help it, can I, if he plays tyrant with his children and raises a traitor under his own nose. I can't change the foreign policy of a nation for a bonbon. What sort of gift?

BEN (*Enters right carrying his gift*) The sentimental sort, Diane.
(YVONNE *exits*)

DIANE (*Seeing it*) A spinning wheel?
(BEN *takes the spinning wheel down left and places it near the fireplace*)

BEN Has a pedal here—you sit here—you push this—

DIANE (*Annoyed*) I know how to spin.

BEN It's been a long time since you made your own clothes. How are you?

DIANE Thriving.

BEN (*Wandering about, peering into things*) A trifle pale, though. Too much in the house of late.

DIANE Mostly your wretched revolution. But then you break in before a person can pinch her cheeks.

BEN Unhealthy life, this. Shouldn't have to pinch 'em if you'd let 'em out in the sun a bit. Bad ventilation. Musty. These old European chateaux have seen their day.

DIANE I can't help you. You know that. What are you after?

BEN (*Indicates the spinning wheel*) Made in Philadelphia.

DIANE Is it? And how are you?

BEN Oh, I'm fit. You know. Busy.

DIANE Gout?

BEN Not so much lately. (*Picks up a silver objet d'art from the mantel*) What'd you pay for this?

DIANE It was a bargain at two hundred francs. Would you like it?

BEN You were robbed, Madame. My friend Paul Revere can turn these out for one-tenth of that.

DIANE What are you selling, Monsieur?

BEN Selling? Just happened to be going by . . . dropped in—pass the time of day—loll on one of your thousand sofas. Is it true you have a thousand sofas?

DIANE More.

BEN Big house to keep clean.

DIANE Will you come to the point?

BEN Where's the kitchen?

DIANE In the east wing.

BEN Where in the east wing?

DIANE (*Bristling*) Somewhere in the east wing.

BEN (*Softly*) You don't know where the kitchen is.

DIANE (*Most sincerely*) Oh, Benjamin, I am sorry about your son.

BEN Stupid of him. Picked the wrong team.

DIANE They'll never make you President now.

BEN S'pose not.

DIANE Your enemies in the Congress will stop the twenty thousand acres of Ohio.

BEN Well, I was going to leave it to Bill, anyway. And Temple's already rich—he's in love.

DIANE (*Warmly*) Did you really come to see me without any purpose whatsoever?

BEN No.

DIANE (*Bristles*) Then what do you want? Recognition is out. Do you think important gifts and flattery from you could so much as make me blink. You can't flatter me, Benjamin. I know you too well.

BEN I can, too, flatter you.

DIANE With effect?

BEN I daresay.

DIANE Flatter me.

BEN All right. I shall try to flatter you. I shall get down
on my bended knee and expose my sincerity.
      (*He kneels*)

DIANE You?

BEN Even me, Madame. Even the best of us come to this.
What can I say of you? Diane! Shall I say that—
      (*Sings "Diane Is"*)
  Like unto—a shop of pretty things,
  Diane is.
  Like unto—a palace full of kings,
  A solid year of springs,
  Diane is, Diane is.
  Like unto—a shelf of books,
  A looking glass of looks,
  A cottage filled with secret nooks,
  My Diane is, my Diane is, my Diane is so—
  But if she never shares it,
  The wealth that is her lot,
  Never ever dares it, to tie a simple knot,
  Then, likely to, is the shop to close,
  The town to doze,
  The year to fly,
  The glass to lie,
  The shelf to turn,
  The cottage to burn which brings

Diane to lonely evenings,
Diane, who once was likened to
A shop of pretty things.

DIANE You flatter me, Franklin, and destroy me, too.

BEN I have not begun to flatter you—and I mean to re-
create whatever I've destroyed before I'm done.

DIANE (*Sits on the sofa*) Alas, Franklin. I wouldn't be a
good wife, I fear. I've loved pleasures too much, too long.

BEN There's nothing wrong with pleasure, my dear Di-
ane. (*Sits on the sofa next to* DIANE) There are all kinds
of pleasures to be had in this life, but one, of course,
should choose amongst them, wisely.
        (*Sings "Look for Small Pleasures"*)
Look for small pleasures
That happen every day,
And not for fortune or fame.
Infinite treasures
Lie all along the way
As do candles waiting for flame.

How simple the joys at our fingertips:
This plain air we share is champagne one sips.

Look for small pleasures
Upon this ball of clay
And not for lightning to tame,
And one day, there's someone,
Just a friendly someone
Who'll be husband or wife to you,
Be the love of all your life to you,

And you'll find how great small pleasures
Can prove.
Will you marry me, Diane?

DIANE (*Turns to* BEN)   Franklin! You *mean* that!!

BEN   I do. I do, indeed.
   (*Sings*)
Who'll be husband or wife to you,
Be the love of all your life to you,
And you'll find how great small pleasures
Can prove.

DIANE   And live in Philadelphia.

BEN   Where every wife's a queen in her own house. But,
   of course, there has to be a Philadelphia to go home to.

DIANE   Oh—ho ho!

BEN   No, no, that invalidates my true emotions not one
   jot.

DIANE   Recognition for you, followed by recognition for
   me.

BEN   Yes.

DIANE   I'll think about it.

BEN   Do!

DIANE   Deeply.

BEN You are tempted?

DIANE Let me say that I love you, Monsieur le Docteur . . .

BEN Thank you, Madame.

DIANE And to share your life would be no hardship, but it is some kind of surrender and I must consider it.

BEN No haste. I'll call on you tomorrow morning.

DIANE Saturday would be my preference.

BEN At the palace.

DIANE You shall have my answer. Till then . . .

BEN Till then. Good afternoon, Madame.
(*He goes to the door*)

DIANE Are you—the most persuasive man on earth?

BEN (*Turning slowly around and with great modesty*) Yes.
(*He goes*)

DIANE (*Sings*)
Diane to lonely evenings,
Diane, who was once likened to
A shop of pretty things.
(YVONNE *enters*)
What is it, Yvonne?

YVONNE   The King has sent his carriage for you, Madame.

DIANE   Send the King his carriage back. And you tell the King I can't see the King just now.

YVONNE   What reason shall I give, Madame?

DIANE   I'm—thinking.

YVONNE   Oui, Madame.
        (YVONNE *exits.* DIANE *turns and stares at the spinning wheel. Slowly she circles it, sits down at it and reacquaints herself with the once familiar mechanism. She begins to spin—an invisible thought*)

DIANE (*Sings*)
    Look for small pleasures
    That happen every day,
    And not for fortune or fame.
    Infinite treasures
    Lie all along the way
    As do candles waiting for flame.

    How simple the joys at our fingertips:
    This plain air we share is champagne one sips.

    Look for small pleasures
    Upon this ball of clay
    And not for lightning to tame,
    And one day there's someone,
    Just a friendly someone,
    Who'll be husband or wife to you,

Be the love of all your life to you,
And you'll find how great small pleasures
Can prove.
  (*She continues to spin as the orchestra plays. The
  lights fade*)

Scene Four

BEN, TEMPLE *and three* MARINES *enter. Two* MARINES
are carrying a printing press; the other MARINE *is carrying a*
wooden box.

BEN   Watch it now, lads. Carry it carefully. If it's too
heavy, just set it down for a minute. And look out for
your toes. (*The* MARINES *set the press down. It drops on*
the toes of one MARINE) Congratulations! (*To* TEMPLE)
Now you see, Temple, moving the press into the study
will make a big difference. There's no light in that shed.
Let me see your latest effort. (TEMPLE *gives him a*
printed page) See what I mean? Not enough ink. Not
enough ink.

TEMPLE   Grandfather, this is ridiculous. There's another
matter I would like—

BEN   A man should have a trade.

TEMPLE   But I'm a lawyer. I would like to—

BEN   Something he does with his hands to earn him a liv-
ing.

TEMPLE   This time in Paris has fitted me out quite well
for a diplomatic post. Now, Grandfather—

BEN Ah, but suppose you're disbarred for your courtroom shenanigans? Suppose your political friends get thrown out of office? You can't practice law and you can't get into an embassy party. What are you going to do? You're a printer. Worse comes to worse, you can print paper money and live on it till they catch you.

TEMPLE And go to jail!

BEN And that's where your diplomatic and legal training will stand you in good stead.

Blackout

Scene Five

Inside BEN's *house at Passy.*

BEN   All right, lads, now lift it up and watch your chins. (*One* MARINE *hits his chin*) It's a good thing I brought you boys over here with me. You'll do less damage on this side of the Atlantic. Now set it down on the table and watch your fingers. (*One* MARINE *sets the printing press on his fingers as they set it on the table*) My boy, up into the kitchen and get a strong cup of coffee. The imminent success of our mission here in France obviously has you bedazzled. (*The* MARINES *exit*) And look out for that step! (*Crash! Offstage*) Minutemen! (*Back to* TEMPLE) All right, Temple, try another!

TEMPLE   Grandfather, please . . .

BEN   Temple, my boy, you, me and the country stand on the treacherous brink of three marriages and it behooves us, lad, to prepare ourselves for the possibility of . . . disaster. Now, put on this apron . . .

TEMPLE   Grandfather, 'tis like a woman's skirt.

BEN   Always look the part. Now the cap . . . (*He has the apron on* TEMPLE *now*) There. A printer if ever I saw one. Anyone would take you for a printer.
    (BEAU *and* CAPTAIN WICKES *enter*)

BEAU (*Seeing* TEMPLE) Well, well—the baker's boy!
(TEMPLE *throws his cap down*)

BEN Bless you, Beau. I can always count on you. Now, Wickes, does the good ship *Reprisal* stand ready to sail us home?

WICKES Aye, Doctor. She lies to, at Calais, whenever you're ready.

BEN I expect the recognition Monday morning. Tuesday we'll quibble about Louisiana. We'll give it to 'em now and buy it back later. And Wednesday morning we sign. Thursday, Temple and I have a double wedding.

BEAU Spoken with the speed of a revolutionist. But, Diane hasn't given you her answer yet and you haven't yet met and approved of Temple's mademoiselle.

BEN Gentlemen, I spent the first thirty years of my life predicting the weather, which made me an expert. When my teeth chatter, I can sagely tell you it's cold out and when a feverish sweat comes over me, I can safely tell you I'm about to get married.

BEAU Benjamin, you are the greatest diplomat in Europe.

BEN Bosh! I didn't do it at the conference table, Beau. I did it in a balloon. I'm no fancy genius. I'm just a boy who knows how to fly a kite.

BEAU But what is the secret of your success?

BEN   Well, my friend, I think the secret lies in the flaw
in my character—for I have lived so long as to have
learned that when you turn a vice into a virtue, you
find your talent! And—

   (*He sings "I Love the Ladies"*)
I love the ladies,
I love them all.
I can make 'em blush
Like Massachusetts in the fall.

I love the ladies,
Their sex I sing.
I can make 'em leap
Like Allegheny creeks in spring.

BEN, BEAU AND WICKES
So let us shoot off cannons
And ring iron bells,
And all down a yard of beer.
For the gentlemen love the ladies,
The ladies love 'em back,
And that's how the devil we're here.

BEAU
I love the ladies,
My mother was one.
And that I have in common
With every other son of a gun.

BEN
I don't adore
A gang of men,
But I enjoy a bevy.

Upon your lap
Who'd want a chap?

ALL

He'd be too bloody heavy!

WICKES

I love the ladies,
Is that a sin?
I can make 'em gay
As Gloucester when the ships come in.

TEMPLE

I love the ladies,
Each one's a poem.
I can make 'em warm
As kitchens in a Hampshire home.

ALL

So let us blow brass trumpets
And beat bass drums
And fiddle at each other's ear,
For the gentlemen love the ladies,
The ladies love 'em back,
And that's how the devil we're here
Yes, sir!
(*Three* MARINES *enter*)

BEN

I love the ladies,
'Tis plain to see
Liberties are what
My politics demand of me.

ALL
Hear! Hear!
Hear! Hear!

MARINES
We love the ladies
From port to port.
Even British girls—

BEN
But only as a last resort!

ALL
So let us shout down rafters
And all stamp our feet
And holler out huzzahs and cheer—huzzah!

BEN, BEAU, WICKES AND TEMPLE
For the gentlemen love the ladies . . .

MARINES
The ladies love them back

ALL
And that's how the devil we're here!
Yes, sir!

TEMPLE, BEAU AND WICKES
We love the ladies,
Heads down to toes,
We can make 'em melt
Like April in the Poconos.

BEN

At every point
Of do or die
Throughout our male existence,
A lady with
A helping hand
Has come to our assistance.

ALL

All together—shout it out for all the world to know!
And if we don't make heaven,
We'll say what the hell!
We've all shared
A first-class berth . . .
Right here!
Where the gentlemen love the ladies,
The ladies love them back,
And that's kind of heaven on earth,
Yes, sir!
That's kind of heaven on earth!

BEN (*Calls*) Jacques!
(JACQUES, *who has appeared on the landing at the end of the song with a tray and glasses of brandy, goes to* BEN. BEN *takes two glasses, gives one to* TEMPLE. JACQUES *gives drinks to* BEAU *and* WICKES)

WICKES Gentlemen, I propose a toast. To the successful culmination of all three weddings.

BEN And Friday, we sail with the evening tide, with three

French ships of war alongside us to blockade the port of New York. (*Raises his glass*) Gentlemen! (*They all drink*) Fill them up again, Jacques!

JACQUES   Pardon, Monsieur le Docteur. That was the last of the brandy.

BEN (*To* TEMPLE)   How's that for budgeting? (*Takes* TEMPLE's *glass and puts it back on* JACQUES' *tray*) This is Jacques Finque, gentlemen, the manager of our household. Jacques, in the year you've been with us, how much did you steal?

JACQUES (*Shocked*)   Monsieur le Docteur, I am an honest man.

BEN   So be honest with me. How much did you steal? Never mind. I'm very fond of you, Jacques. Even though you are Lord Stormont's spy.

JACQUES (*Caught*)   I protest.

WICKES   You mean you've known all along this man to be the British Ambassador's spy and yet you've kept him on in this house?

TEMPLE   That's my grandfather!

BEN   Always like to know where the enemy is. That's all, Jacques. Merci, merci. (JACQUES *goes up the stairs, exits*) Besides he's a damn good servant and since Stormont's been paying him he didn't cost so much. How's *that* for budgeting?

BENNY (*Comes tumbling down the stairs*) Grandfather! Grandfather! Who's the pretty girl upstairs in Temple's room?

TEMPLE (*To* BEN) That's what I've been trying to tell you, sir, for one hour, since I came back from Paris, but you don't listen to what you fail to think is important.

BEN I'm sorry.

TEMPLE (*Goes to* BENNY) Benny, would you fetch her down here, please?

BENNY Gladly and by the hand.
(*He goes up the stairs and exits*)

BEN *That* boy's a boy after my own heart.

TEMPLE (*To* BEN) Now, this wench is going to be my wife, sir.

BEN Yes, yes.

TEMPLE If you don't like her terribly much, when the war's won, we'll live in Boston.

BEN As you wish.

TEMPLE But if she and I have children, they will some-day be your great grandchildren. So I solicit your total attention, for the next ten minutes, to this minor business, called my life.

BEN Damn it . . . (BENNY *and* JANINE *enter*) you're a rotten salesman. I've developed quite a loathing for the

girl since you've been talking. Wickes, you give a boy
his head and he'll—
    (*Stops and stares at his friend from the Spanish
    Embassy garden*)

JANINE (*Softly*) I told you, Monsieur le Docteur, that
one day you would know me very well.

BEN Where are my twelve guns?

JANINE I brought them.
    (JANINE *goes into* BEN's *extended arms*)

BEN For whom you'd gamble with your life and nothing
less?

JANINE Oui. 'Tis whom I meant. And (*Proving she reads
him*) "The devil wipes his nose with poor men's pride."

BEN It has lost something in the translating. But this child
belongs in *my* family!

JANINE (*Conveying the memory of their mutual secret*)
Shall we dance, Monsieur le Docteur, as if we had once
danced before?

BEN My pleasure, Mademoiselle. (*They dance to the
music of the waltz, "When I Dance with the Person I
Love." There is a knock at the door*) Jacques!
    (JACQUES *enters and goes to the door as* BEN *and*
    JANINE *dance.* JACQUES *re-enters carrying the spin-
    ning wheel*)

JACQUES Monsieur le Docteur . . .

BEN   Where'd that come from?
(BEN *turns* JANINE *over to* BEAU, *who dances with her, then* WICKES *twirls her about—then,* TEMPLE)

JACQUES (*Aside, to* BEN)   From Madame de Vobrillac, Monsieur le Docteur. He, who brought it, said it was an answer of a kind—that you would understand.

BEN   Yes, I do, indeed. Well, that's that. (JACQUES *starts to go up the stairs*) Jacques . . . (JACQUES *stops*) Tell Lord Stormont that I have decided to make that little channel trip and pack my bags, will you? Have the carriage readied and brought 'round. And not a word of this.

JACQUES   Monsieur le Docteur—don't. They mean to kill you.

BEN   Jacques, you're a rotten spy. Go on, now. Quick.
(JACQUES *goes up the stairs, taking* BENNY *with him.* BEN *picks up his cane and climbs the stairs*)

TEMPLE (*Calling across the room as he waltzes with* JANINE)   Grandfather, isn't she wonderful?

BEN (*On the landing*)   Aye, laddy, we Franklins, we are lucky men. For you know the girl you love and I, at last, know "the girl" I love.
(BEN *exits and the lights fade on* TEMPLE *and* JANINE *dancing and* BEAU *looking at the spinning wheel, with a growing suspicion that something has gone wrong*)

Curtain

Scene Six

A corridor at Versailles. A FOOTMAN *enters, followed by*
BEN. DIANE *enters from the other side.*

BEN Bonjour, Madame la Comtesse. (*The* FOOTMAN
exits) I came to say until we meet again. I'm taking a
little trip. When I get back I'll tell you all about it. Going to Prussia. May get them to do something.

DIANE My spies tell me you are going to London.

BEN Well, I've got a lot of old friends in London.

DIANE You have a lot of old enemies there, too.

BEN Lady, I've small choice!

DIANE I can't help that!

BEN I appreciate the fact that you cannot help that. I've
no quarrel with you.

DIANE Let it go, Benjamin. Let younger men fight the battle. You've earned things you should have now—private
peace, rewards.

BEN Why'd you send me back the spinning wheel?

DIANE It isn't me you love.

BEN I do though. Privately.

DIANE But you're not a private man.

BEN We're all public men when the issue is liberty, Madame.

DIANE Did they guarantee you safe conduct?

BEN Oh, surely.

DIANE (*Turns to* BEN) They'll hang you the minute you step off the boat.

BEN Cause a hullabaloo in France if they do.

DIANE (*Really shocked*) Mon dieu! A martyr. So that's the game. Oh, Benjamin, that's not like you. That's not —*practical*.

BEN I consulted with my liver the other day—and it's not too long for this world, anyway.

DIANE Benjamin!

BEN Dearest . . . friend. Now you listen—we'll meet in heaven someday—and—they'll have winter rain and chess up there, I feel quite certain. And they'll give us each a pair of wings and we'll . . .

(Sings)
Sail the skies
Off to the farthest little star we'll go.
Sail the skies
And watch the people disappear below.

I'll stop and smile
Because for all the rest of time,
I'll know
　　(Spoken)
I'll be alone with you.

DIANE   Don't go, yet. Don't go, just yet.

BEN   I've a restless British Ambassador outside.

DIANE   Well, you'll—want to say goodbye to Louis. 'Tis protocol.

BEN   If you wish.

DIANE   I'll arrange it, Monsieur.

BEN   The million francs was a tremendous help.

DIANE *(Pause, and then softly)*   Life for a lost cause, Ben?

BEN *(With firm, quiet conviction)*   It will happen. I believe it.

DIANE   Oui. I see you do.
　　(She starts to exit)

BEN (*Stops her*) If you don't mind, I'd rather not go into that damned Throne Room with that fancy footman going bang, bang, and hollering "Franklin of Philadelphia."

DIANE What would you rather he say?

BEN Nothing. I'd rather he said nothing, since he cannot say what I'd rather he say.

DIANE I'll do what I can, Monsieur.
(*She exits*)

BEN (*To himself, simply*) I have heard about a cask of good Madeira wine into which a small fly fell, which cask was corked and shipped three thousand miles across the sea, where after twenty years of lying in the dark, it was brought up, was opened, and a first glass filled from it, at which filling, it chanced that a small drop of wine was spilled upon the table top and in that drop lay the self-same fly, who, seeming dead, did, as the sun shone and dried his wings, arise miraculously and shook himself and flew up bustling into the blue day as alive again as ever he had been! I don't know how scientific that tale is, but I should like to be buried in such a cask of good Madeira wine that after two hundred years I, too, should rise up and stand once more on Pennsylvania land and walk and talk and breathe the free air, for I know in my heart somehow it will be free. I know it. I know it even now! What a dream! Two hundred years. And I wonder. I wonder how I'd find them then—those Americans to whom the name American will not be new. Will they love liberty, being given it outright in the crib for nothing? Will they know that if you are not free, you are, sir, lost without hope, and will they who reaped that harvest of ideas be willing to strive to preserve what we so willingly strove to plant? That all men are created equal! And are endowed by their creator with certain in-alienable rights. Yes, and would they die for it? That's the question one finally has to ask oneself. Would I die for it! And the answer one has to say—is—yes, sir, I would!

(*A* FOOTMAN *enters*)

FOOTMAN   Monsieur le Docteur, the King will see you now.

BEN   Yes . . . I'll be right along. (*The* FOOTMAN *exits.* BEN *starts off, saying to the audience as he goes*) Well, anyway, it would be fun to be pickled for two hundred years in a cask of good Madeira wine!

Blackout

SCENE SEVEN

The Hall of Mirrors at Versailles. The room is filled with people—the entire court. The King is on the throne. DIANE *is to his left.* BEN *enters. The* FOOTMAN *stomps his staff three times.*

BEN   Damn! There he goes again.

FOOTMAN (*In a ringing voice*)   Monsieur le Docteur, Benjamin Franklin . . . the Ambassador of the United States of America!
>   (*The music of the opening barcarole plays under. It is a memory of the States.* BEN, *taken completely by surprise, weeps. The man who invented himself weeps. All the ladies curtsy—the men bow. And last of all,* DIANE *curtsies as if to say "I did it for you" and the nation is born*)

Slow Curtain